GEORGES ROUAULT'S
M I S E R E R E

SELF-PORTRAIT, Georges Rouault (1871–1958). Lithograph. 1926.
Rosenwald Collection, National Gallery of Art, Washington, D. C.

GEORGES ROUAULT'S
MISERERE

FRANK and DOROTHY GETLEIN

THE BRUCE PUBLISHING COMPANY
MILWAUKEE

NIHIL OBSTAT:
> JOHN F. MURPHY, S.T.D.
> *Censor librorum*

IMPRIMATUR:
> ✝ WILLIAM E. COUSINS
> *Archbishop of Milwaukee*
> April 26, 1963

We are deeply grateful to Lessing J. Rosenwald, Elizabeth Mongan, former curator of the Rosenwald Collection and Katharine Shepard, Assistant Print Curator of the National Gallery of Art, Washington, D. C.

Specifically Georges Rouault, *Miserere et Guerre* Plates 1–58 (aquatint, etching, heliogravure, and other methods), also the *Self-Portrait, Léon Bloy,* and *André Suarès* (lithographs), National Gallery of Art, Washington, D. C., Rosenwald Collection.

Library of Congress Catalog Card Number: 63–19633

TO
Leonard Scheller

CONTENTS

GUERRE

GEORGES ROUAULT

In 1905 Paris could still be shocked by art, and in 1905 Paris was shocked profoundly by an exhibition of young painters who were immediately called the "Fauves," or wild beasts. The artists have since become leaders in the art of the twentieth century. Among them were Henri Matisse, Maurice Vlaminck, André Derain, and Georges Braque. The Fauve paintings do not shock us today because their artistic vocabulary has long been part of the visual language of art. Understanding this vocabulary, we have no trouble in seeing at once that the whole Fauve movement was primarily an enthusiastic expression of great joy in life, in the earth, and in art.

The very elements which shocked the Paris of 1905 we respond to immediately as to a glad hymn. The Fauves drastically simplified the forms of nature and made up for this simplification by becoming even more drastic in their use of bright colors. We look at the sea made of hundreds of tiny strokes of purest blue, at trees which seem to dance in the bright green paint, at foliage in red and orange rivaling the sunset colors. We accept this as pure delight in the life of things.

But there was another painter among the Fauves whose paintings shocked for other reasons. The scene of the shocking works was the Salon d'Automne, an annual event founded a few years earlier by these painters. Because the exhibition was in the autumn it may be supposed that much of the bright, singing color came from the color of summer. Many of the paintings were the product not only of the summer but of the summer spent on the southern coast of France. In some of the paintings, surely, what shocked Paris was the unexpected impact of the southern sun, the force of the Mediterranean released under cool Paris skies. But that other painter, who fit in with the Fauves no more than the Fauves fit in with ordinary, academic art, did not sing in his work of summer sun and the joy of the fruitful earth. He confronted exhibition visitors with dark pictures of baleful shapes; threatening skies above stripped, blasted landscapes, briefly seen as the background for

1

the bloated, monstrous figures: beastly creatures dressed as judges of France; clowns, faces cracked, the gloom of the picture sometimes split, as if by lightning, by livid yellow spangles on their grotesque, circus clothes; hideous women and more hideous couples, staring insolently at the spectator.

This painter was Georges Rouault.

Despite his emotional use of color, despite his free distortion of figures, Rouault was not really related to the Fauve movement, so short-lived yet so influential in twentieth-century painting. He was then and remained most of his life a solitary in his art, joining no movements, member of no school, going his own way, faithful to the memory of his teacher, Gustave Moreau, whose work his own in no way resembled; faithful, too, to the friendship and teaching of Léon Bloy, who never understood the art of Georges Rouault.

It is a mistake to confuse the life of an artist with his work. Nevertheless it is true that nothing appears in the work without having passed through the life in one way or another: from the actual perception of a closely copied flower in a landscape to the consciousness of God's creative force on the Sistine ceiling. The life of Georges Rouault reveals many of the themes that appear over and over in his work; and eventually there comes a period when the work itself seems to be the life, providing, among other things, that steady quota of personal suffering which shaped so profoundly his art. That period and that continuing work of art were the *Miserere* series of prints. Begun in 1914, at the start of World War I, the great series — still only somewhat more than half of the original plan — was not published until 1948. The *Miserere* thus occupied thirty years of the artist's maturity. Most of the subjects of his other paintings appear in the *Miserere* prints and it is unquestionable that his fully mature style in painting is related to the agonizing methods he followed or invented in the making of the plates from which the prints were to be made for the *Miserere*.

The series was begun in war; so was Rouault's life. Moreover, it was the peculiarly ironic kind of war — social as well as military — that was to appear as a regular feature of the *Miserere;* such a war, indeed, was the original thought behind what were to have been fifty plates in a series of one hundred.

2

Rouault was born in Belleville, a working-class suburb of Paris, on May 27, 1871. He was born in a cellar, where his mother had taken refuge from the bombardment of Paris. The city was being shelled and it was being shelled by French troops.

This bitter struggle of Frenchman against Frenchman — destined to be repeated in the darkest days of World War II — had come about through social and political circumstances which again relate closely to the major themes of Rouault's art. The French Second Empire of the preposterous emperor, Napoleon III, had rashly sought the old Napoleonic *gloire* in war with Prussia. Under Bismarck the Prussian military state was about to become a German empire even more preposterous than that of Napoleon III, but the German venture, like the Prussian, would be in deadly earnest and in deadly, total efficiency. The thoroughly rehearsed Prussian army ran over the ill-prepared French Imperial troops in record time, captured the charlatan "emperor of the French," deposed him, took Paris, proclaimed their own emperor, dictated peace, and withdrew. The overthrow of Napoleon III required about half the summer of 1870.

At this point both the Germans and the French Imperialists assumed the war was over. They had forgotten one thing: the French people. The city of Paris particularly rallied around the old battle cry of the Republic and fought savagely against the invading Germans. The war dragged on until January, 1871, when it became clear that superior force would have its way. In Versailles, the seat of the old French kings, the Germans proclaimed their emperor and exacted the provinces of Alsace and Lorraine from France as the price of having been duped by the nephew of Napoleon I.

Four months before Rouault's birth, there were therefore set up several of the conditions which would dominate Europe for almost the whole of his lifetime. Foremost was the bitter Franco-German rivalry. To the French, as indeed to most of the world, the old image of the German as scholarly, or gemütlich, or scientific, or philosophic, was gone forever.

The seizure of Alsace-Lorraine, of course, became the permanent and poignant French symbol of German injustice throughout the first fifty years of Rouault's life. The provinces were recovered by France at the end of World War I, again annexed by Germany after the Nazi triumph of 1940, and again recovered by France in 1945.

Meanwhile, profound bitterness and dissatisfaction were coming to the surface in French domestic, economic, and political life. The chief social significance of Louis Napoleon's tragicomic empire had been the unleashing upon France of a greedy swarm of financial speculators who brought the industrial revolution to a climax of achievement and helped create the image of predatory capitalism at its worst. Against these exploiters, French workers were very slow to gain any protection at all. Financial scandals, government corruption, and industrial exploitation were to mark the history of France until the eve of World War II.

After the defeat in war of Napoleon III and after a Royalist provisional government made peace with the triumphant Germans, Paris, with several of the other larger cities, revolted and established communes, a system of democratic government that goes back to the Middle Ages. The French provisional government, operating at Versailles, opened war on the people of Paris. Government troops bombarded the city, fought their way in and, eventually, slaughtered out of hand some tens of thousands of Paris citizens, men, women, and children.

During these dread events, Georges Rouault was born in a Belleville cellar, his mother sheltering from the passionate politics that ended the Second Empire and set the tone for the Third Republic.

Rouault was born into a family of craftsmen, an economic class that suffered particularly during the long change of the French economy from individual to mass production. His father was a cabinetmaker employed in a piano factory. Owing perhaps to the circumstances of his birth, the baby was weak and sickly and was not expected to survive infancy. Against such a fatalistic attitude, the baby's maternal grandmother, Mme. Champdovaine, set her hand. The grandmother arranged a program of special feeding and tender care, under which the boy, living for long periods at his grandparents' house, gained strength.

Grandfather Champdovaine was a great admirer of the new artists of nineteenth-century France, especially of Manet, whose prints he collected. Also in the Champdovaine household, the boy Rouault en-

4

countered the substance of paint for the first time. He was allowed to play with the materials with which his aunts practiced the contemporary ladies' amusement of decorating fans and china.

In boyhood, too, Rouault learned what a terribly complicated thing religion can be when it is mixed with politics. The Catholic Church in France had been thoroughly involved with politics ever since the fifth-century baptism of Clovis, king of the Franks. In the late nineteenth century, although very slowly and very painfully withdrawing from direct political involvement, the Church was reaping a harvest of hatred and of indifference on the part of many Frenchmen as a result of centuries-long association with one group of oppressors after another.

But under the influence of the liberal philosopher Lammenais there was spreading at the same time the notion that Catholicism could be as effectively committed to the idea of freedom in political life as it had once been to the authority and rights of kings. When Lammenais was condemned by Pius IX, Rouault's father, who was deeply committed to this new view of Catholicism in France, immediately enrolled the boy in a Protestant school as a gesture of disapproval.

Formal education did not last long. When Georges was severely punished in class, his father decided against education and in favor of the traditional training of French artisans. He apprenticed Rouault, at the age of fourteen, to a stained-glass maker. By the end of the apprenticeship, which lasted six years, Rouault had found his lifework: he would be an artist.

Much has been made of the influence on Rouault's painting of his apprentice years in a stained-glass studio — probably too much. His fully mature style, taken together with his religious subjects, immediately suggests the medieval glasswork at Chartres and the other great cathedrals. Rouault in his paintings often heightened the glowing colors by thick bands of black paint separating them; these bands strike the superficial gaze as resembling the bands of lead with which medieval glass was held together. The lead bars in the glass, however, were an absolute physical necessity in order to hold together the broad expanses of glass in the twelfth century, just as the flying buttresses of the cathedrals were not arrived at as decoration but as vital structural members in a daring architectural effort.

What Rouault did pick up in the stained-glass studios was a personal application of the ingrained integrity of the French craftsman. That, much more than the look of stained glass, was the medieval heritage of Georges Rouault. That heritage of honest craftsmanship acquired by training as a decorative artisan came into French modern art through three great artists: Renoir of the preceding generation, Rouault, and Georges Braque, his companion for a short time as a Fauve. But the medieval heritage was more a matter of outlook upon work and life than it was of visual resemblance.

The training also confirmed his lifelong revulsion at certain aspects of modern life as they were emerging even then. Years later he wrote in horror at having seen "mere chromolithographs on glossy paper slipped between two panes of leaded glass."

The apprenticeship in stained glass also brought him into daily contact with religious subjects. Thus, from the age of fourteen to that of twenty, as he grew gradually in art and craftsmanship he accepted religion as a perfectly natural subject for art. This was against the grain of virtually all advanced French painters of the nineteenth century and was to be more so during the twentieth. In this, painting shared the assumptions of most fields of intellectual activity. For bright young French artists, poets, novelists, scientists, and politicians, the Christian faith, for so many centuries an intimate part of the reality of France, had simply ceased to be very important. It was to be part of Rouault's achievement that he revealed for many the relevance of Christianity to what has been called the "post-Christian" era.

As an apprentice he became more and more attracted to painting, more and more determined to give up his apprenticeship and enroll as an art student in the Ecole des Beaux-Arts. His craftsman father was horrified. He had planned and worked to ensure that his dreamy son would have in his hands the means of livelihood. Furthermore, his choice of a trade for the boy seemed especially good because there was a great revival in the use of stained glass, a revival destined to continue for decades. And the family could well use the wages the apprentice was now bringing home.

The youth's mother took his side. Mme. Rouault not only argued his case against his father, she went out of the home and took various

6

jobs herself to supply the deficit in the family income which would result from Georges's quitting his apprenticeship and becoming an art student. In 1891, he enrolled at the Beaux-Arts; a few months later his teacher died and Rouault was entered in the studio of Gustave Moreau, an artist who was to have a permanent effect on the growing painter.

Although in recent years there has been some revival of interest in Moreau, he is still all but unknown outside art historian circles. At the time Rouault entered his painting class, however, Moreau was an important and well-known French painter. Also, he was quite deliberately a painter of religious themes. In Gustave Moreau's painting, Christianity was the plastic equivalent of what it became in the novels of J.-K. Huysmans: an exotic survival of an exotic past, romantic and colorful, mysterious and linked historically with the mist-shrouded beginnings of Europe. In reaction against a dull, materialistic, vulgar age, the age of the stock manipulators, Huysmans and other French and English literary men of the period cultivated first an incredible revival of Satanism, complete with Black Masses, and then a "rediscovered" Catholicism, more medieval than the Middle Ages. Whatever Moreau's personal understanding of Christianity, his religious pictures were the fitting illustration of Huysmans' passages of religious faith. Figures strike romantic poses. Strange lights glisten out of soft darkness. The episodes and personages of the Gospel have become material for a pantomime.

Moreau, however, would have been the last to insist that his own example, either religious or artistic, was the one to be followed blindly by his students. He was a good teacher, on the watch for signs of talent, however differently they might express themselves. Matisse was a member of the class, along with Rouault.

Under the tolerant instruction of Moreau, the young man mastered the techniques of academic drawing and of academic painting. There was nothing especially personal in his work — as there certainly was in Moreau's — but the faults disappeared, too, and he became, by the time he was twenty-two, a remarkably competent student. He was the favorite student of Moreau and at the master's suggestion he submitted a large-scale work in a major competition, for the Prix-de-Rome. The picture was *Samson at the Mill,* and might have been painted by any

7

of a dozen competent academic painters in Paris at the time. It failed to win a prize.

In 1894, however, he won a major prize and another the following year. Again he entered the competition for the Prix-de-Rome and failed. His entry was a large and conventional *Christ Mourned by the Holy Women*. The equally conventional picture of the year before, *The Child Jesus among the Doctors,* was destined to be purchased almost a quarter of a century later, when Rouault's style had long been removed from the academic, by the government of France.

After his second failure to win the Prix-de-Rome, Moreau advised Rouault to leave the Ecole des Beaux-Arts. The student had learned all the master could teach. Henceforth he must teach himself.

The two men remained friends. Moreau died in 1898 and did a touching thing in his will. He left his studio, full of pictures, at the time of great value, to France as a museum but he stipulated that his favorite pupil be made curator. From that point on Rouault was the curator of the Gustave Moreau Museum with a salary of roughly $300 a month. Moreau, having urged him to follow his own path, had in death made it possible for him to do so.

It was not an easy path to find, let alone follow. Rouault continued his steady perfection of his academic style. In 1900, he was awarded a bronze medal at the Paris World's Fair, indicating his mastery of acceptable art in the century just ended; what haunted Rouault was the direction his art would take in the century just begun. Whatever that art would be, it would almost certainly be tied closely with whatever Christianity would be for the young artist. Catholic Christianity in France at the turn of the century was giving extraordinary signs of discovering new life. All reasonable predictions were that the Church was all but dead, as dead as the old French monarchy with which it had so long fought and with which it had so long been allied. Marx had said religion was the opiate of the people, but in France this had ceased to be true, at least in the cities, certainly in Paris. The masses, the working people, were in the midst of a long drift away from the Church of their fathers, a drift that is today very widespread. The old monarchy was, as it still is, utterly irrelevant to French life, hence of no meaningful support to the Church. Whatever social reality French

Catholicism had, seemed to be an adjunct and an ornament of bourgeois life. Middle-class women went to Mass and cultivated a rigorous personal piety, a piety not entirely free of surviving Jansenism, the French Puritanical heresy. But in the midst of this there were signs of life stirring once more, as it had so often, within what were easily taken to be the dead bones of Christianity.

One sign of life through the late nineteenth century was the revival of the Benedictine Order and with it, through Dom Gueranger, the reawakening of interest in the liturgy of the Church. The revived Benedictines at times took on certain fashionable appeal and reached their peak of exotic interest when, for a brief period, it seemed that J.-K. Huysmans was on the point of associating himself with the Order, on terms never quite made clear. Early in the new century Rouault met Huysmans and the famous, professionally decadent, now palpitatingly Catholic, writer seems to have made little impression upon the searching artist, despite the poet's keen appreciation of the qualities of Moreau, Rouault's beloved teacher. Whatever Rouault's Christian art was to be, it would not be the visual manifestation of Huysmans' medievalistic Catholicism. For one thing, Moreau himself had already done that job. For another, Rouault belonged to a younger generation.

In 1903, however, he met another consciously Catholic writer who affected him tremendously and whose influence, in spite of the writer himself, can certainly be seen in Rouault's work of the next few years and to some extent in his work of the next half century.

This was Léon Bloy, the self-styled "Pilgrim of the Absolute," not a very finished writer of the narrative fiction he attempted, certainly not a very balanced theologian, but utterly possessed by the love of Jesus. He felt with an intensity that struck many as deranged, the absolute value of Christian poverty, the path of suffering as the only human way toward union with Christ. He despised and denounced the middle-class social order, with its blindness to the economic misery it produced, and especially he cried out against the lightning-stroke revelations of the Gospel being reduced to ornaments of the decorous life of middle-class ladies.

He was, from the point of view of most Christians in France, both clerical and lay, a thoroughly objectionable character, possibly demented, and certainly given to sweeping exaggeration in his claims for what he called the absolute and in his resolute refusal to find the slightest shred of virtue in the lives of bourgeois Christians. Here at last was no ultrarefined retreat from present realities to the remembered glories of the medieval Church. Here, rather, was an impassioned confrontation between the message of the Gospels, in its most extreme interpretation, and the total failure of what still called itself a Christian society to come anywhere close to living that Gospel. Here, also, was a burning renewal of the ancient Christian personal charity, a love going out indiscriminately to all the destitute.

Rouault was fascinated by Léon Bloy. He met him first in his books, especially *The Woman Who Was Poor*. Raissa Maritain has described the effect of reading this violent Jeremiad novel, for herself and for Jacques Maritain: "For the first time we found ourselves before the reality of Christianity. Up to that time . . . something, I do not know what, masked me from Christianity's real being, placing it in some realm of art and imagination. Reading [*The Woman Who Was Poor*] we passed through the literary form . . . to the man, the man of faith illumined by rays of that strange thing, so unknown to us — Catholicism — and, so to speak, identified with it."

On Rouault, Bloy had a similar effect. Here was the faith in Jesus come out of the decorous pictures of the Academy, out of such pictures as Rouault himself had submitted for the Prix-de-Rome, and into the steaming, smelly, wicked streets of modern Paris. Such a conception of Christianity demanded a new pictorial language. Rouault was not long in making it.

At the same time the financially secure museum curator was noticing the city life around him and noticing, as one will, how closely it corresponded with the city Bloy wrote about. Paris at the turn of the century was, after all, still the Paris of the Impressionists: Renoir had almost two decades of work ahead of him, Monet more than a quarter of a century. But the aspect of Paris that so illumines their joyful paintings and through their paintings lives still for us — that pleasant prospect of the City of Light — seems never to have registered on Rouault. He saw a different Paris.

He saw the Parisian prostitutes, not as glamorous creatures dancing

10

the cancan in Montmartre cafes, but as exploited, ruined souls, worthy of infinite pity. He saw the down-and-outs of the city lounging around the streets. He saw the unthinking cruelty of the courts to the poor — decades earlier, another Parisian, Anatole France, had said, "The Law, in its majestic equality, forbids all men to sleep under bridges, to beg in the streets and to steal bread, the rich as well as the poor." He saw particularly the pathetic efforts of marginal entertainers — jugglers, clowns, acrobats — to bring a moment's cheer to others out of the misery of their own lives. He looked at the Paris around him and saw the Paris of Léon Bloy. For a travelogue through this limbo, again, a new pictorial language was needed.

He became one of a circle of intellectual Catholics that centered on Léon Bloy. Jacques and Raissa Maritain were of the group and have reported that Rouault listened more than he talked. Bloy has projected the fictional figure of a Christian artist which seems to describe the young Rouault perfectly and Jacques Maritain has recorded that the ideal of a Christian artist, set forth in *Art and Scholasticism,* is Rouault. For his part Rouault acknowledged his debt to Bloy by attempting to illustrate two of the most frightful characters in *The Woman Who Was Poor,* M. and Mme. Poulot, who persecuted the saintly heroine.

Then a strange thing began to happen. Partly through Bloy, Rouault, in his early thirties, was finding the path in faith and art that he was to follow for half a century. In his art he was to bring from the Christian faith a message of compassion to the post-Christian world of the twentieth century, a world already convinced, on widespread evidence, that "God is dead." To the Christian faith itself he was to bring the peculiar illumination that only great artists do bring and that had been sadly absent from the faith for over two centuries. In all of this achievement, Léon Bloy played a memorable part. And as that achievement began, Bloy publicly and privately disowned and disavowed his disciple.

Bloy to begin with was happy to add the young Rouault to his handful of followers. In his journal, in 1904, he recorded the painter's enthusiasm for *The Woman Who Was Poor:* "My book has touched him to the quick and left a wound that will never heal. I tremble to think of the sufferings in store for the unfortunate man." Bloy himself was to inflict some of the suffering, and that soon.

11

Leon Bloy

In the following year the author got around to visiting the Moreau Museum, where Rouault modestly displayed some of his own work along with that of his teacher. Bloy was especially taken with the ten-year-old set piece, *The Child Jesus Among the Doctors*. He wrote, "I didn't realize that Rouault had an immense talent. I realize it now and have told him so enthusiastically." Rouault already, and partly in response to Bloy, had left the manner of *The Child Jesus* far behind. His new art, to some extent inspired by Bloy, could not be merely illustrations of the author's views. Rather, Rouault experienced in his own way, a visual way, what for Bloy was narrative and abstract proposition. It was a radical departure from the traditional painting he had been doing and the change was too much for Bloy.

Six months later the writer visited the Salon d'Automne of 1905 and was shocked. "It's a sorry sight. He's seeking a new path, what a pity! This artist apparently capable of painting the angels now does nothing else but the most shocking and vindictive caricatures. Bourgeois foulness has wrought so violent and horrified a reaction in him that his art seems to have received the deathblow."

In reality, of course, Rouault's art had just been born.

The savage figures of hulking prostitutes, mirthless clowns, and men and women bereft of pity disturbed Bloy and they disturbed others. These figures from the Parisian jungle were accompanied, sometimes, by a head of Christ, painted with the same disregard of academic precepts, the same use of the paint strokes themselves to express the infinite sorrow of the subject. In 1908 Rouault spent days attending court sessions and painting his first series of judges. In that year also he married Marthe Le Sidaner, a musician. They were to have four children.

The newly married husband had little enough prospect of success in his chosen field. The Cubist revolution had already begun. In a few short years it would be a raging fashion, attracting hundreds of artists willing to turn out cheap versions of the pure forms created by Picasso and Braque. Rouault distorted forms freely enough, but in his own way, for his own purposes. The last thing in the world that interested him was the pure aesthetic of the Cubists. He was making his own new art, composed of new technical means and new artistic vision fused into a

13

single thing with a new discovery of a message two thousand years old. The combination was enough to frighten off both those Parisians who were interested in any new form of art and those others, the Christians, who might have been interested in religious art. If there was no immediate prospect of a market for Rouault's painting, it didn't stop him. He had the appointment at the Moreau Museum and it was enough for a modest independence. The painter, finding his own way through completely unexplored territory, was thirty-eight years old before he had his first one-man show in Paris, an event which is nowadays normally administered by twenty-five.

War came to interrupt the humble pursuit of truth and at the same time to reveal to Rouault the most horrible state of modern life. The coming of war also had immediate and drastic effects on the small fixed income the little family lived on. It shrank before their eyes as prices of all commodities rose to meet the wartime demand for food, for clothing, for shelter, even for the materials of painting. It occurred to Rouault that he must give up his art and find employment of some kind, but his wife, like his mother years before, had a total belief in the worth of what he was doing. Before marriage she had been a professional musician of considerable promise. She redeemed the promise now. She gave lessons on the piano and the fees from her students kept the family eating and Rouault painting.

Meanwhile the determining and crucial force was moving into the life of Georges Rouault. His exhibitions had not set Paris on its ear. They had not been sellouts. But one dealer was interested, the strange figure of Ambroise Vollard, a man intimately involved in the progress of modern art, from the Impressionists to the Surrealists and after. In America an art dealer normally represents an artist on a commission basis, the commission normally being one third of the price of pictures, this third taking care of overhead in the gallery, of mailings and other publicity, of expenses incurred in the actual selling of pictures, and, finally, of profit. In Paris this system is not generally followed and it was not at all that of Ambroise Vollard.

Like most French art dealers handling the work of living artists he regarded himself not as an artist's representative but as a merchant, buying goods for as little as he could, selling them for as much as he

14

could. He became interested in Rouault through some faces the artist had painted and glazed on ceramic. He then proposed to buy all the pictures in Rouault's studio. The proposition was a gift from heaven to the young family in its difficulties. Yet Rouault hesitated. There were perhaps seven hundred paintings in the studio. The artist, an extremely slow and painstaking worker who approved his own work even more slowly, did not want what he thought of as unfinished paintings to be presented to the world. Vollard agreed not to exhibit or resell anything until it had the artist's approval and his signature. As the war went on, their formal relationship changed again. Vollard became Rouault's sole dealer, the owner, for resale, of all works of which Rouault approved. Once more, financial security had come from nowhere, unexpectedly, and firmly established Rouault as a practicing artist with no need to do other work. Vollard was happy enough to pay Rouault a regular salary, enough to support the family, without too close regard to immediate return on his money. If it is said of such art dealers that they drive a shrewd bargain, it must also be said that they do recognize new artistic value before other eyes can perceive it and that they back their own recognitions with their own cash.

Vollard was more than an art dealer. He was also an *animateur*, which is to say an impressario, one who saw ways in which artists could be put to work to the profit of all concerned, not least the purely artistic growth and achievement of the artist. Modestly at first and then with increasing ambition, Vollard had begun the business of fine-art publishing. Nowadays that means mostly books of reproductions of paintings. For Vollard and for a few other European *animateurs* of this century, the term meant much more than that. It meant conceiving and bringing to reality a print project for a specified artist. Usually this went no further than matching a contemporary artist's style to some literary classic, often a new translation from Latin or Greek or a new, and invariably limited, edition of one of the great French poems, novels, or dramas. Often, too, the involvement of the artist was limited to the creation of a series of drawings for the project. The making of the plates and the printing of them was turned over to highly skilled craftsmen.

Whether printed by the artist or printed by a craftsman from the artist's plates, prints — etchings, engravings, woodcuts, lithographs —

André Suarès

are original works of art. The original is not the copper, stone or wood, but every impression made from them on paper. Hence, Vollard was often involved in artistic creation as well as the merchandising of art.

Considering how best to use this strange new artist he had added to his group, Vollard hit upon not one but two books. The dealer was by now intimately familiar with all of Rouault's production — after all, it all belonged to him once it was finished. Having an extremely sensitive mind and an extremely sensitive eye, Vollard was probably the first person to grasp the potential achievement of Georges Rouault. True to the highest tradition of the *animateur* dealer, he may well have seen better than the artist where his path was leading. He proposed two books, not of drawings to illustrate a text, but really of pictures themselves with texts to illustrate them. The texts were to be written by Rouault's poet friend, André Suarès, but, as the project dragged on endlessly over the years, this was never done. The first volume was to be *Miserere,* a theme suggested by the whole body of Rouault's work so far; the second volume was to be drawn from the experience through which they were living and was to be called *Guerre,* or *War.* Rouault agreed; Vollard agreed. Almost at once there began a staggering sequence of misunderstandings, mistakes from which there was no drawing back, apparently fruitless labor endured for years. The relationship with Vollard was a determining one for Rouault and within that relationship the making of the *Miserere* was the central fact.

From Rouault's first conceptions for such a print series, in 1913, to his final publishing of the series, in 1948, thirty-five years elapsed, enough to bring a man from infancy to maturity, from youth to the grave. The prints stretch across Rouault's life like a great watershed. They shaped almost all his work. For years he thought about them in pure frustration, believing that he had given his soul to a project which would never see the light of day. From them, however, he brought forth not only most of the images of his painting but even the style, the manner, the experiences of painting, unlikely as that must seem to one who knows the difference between a painting and a print.

The process began with dispatch. There were to be fifty pictures for each of the two volumes. Rouault set to work and made drawings in India ink. At this point the project, or at least his participation in it, could have been at an end, for many an art publisher would have been happy to have drawings and would have known how to use them to make a handsome book. Not Vollard. He felt that Rouault really showed himself to best advantage not as a draftsman but as a painter, and this was true. He handed back the drawings with the request that they be redone as paintings suitable for printmaking.

Rouault took his work and began the process of making it into paintings. Again, when this was completed, many publishers would have stopped there and arranged very easily to have the paintings reproduced. Again, not Vollard. He had the paintings mechanically engraved, by the process of heliogravure, into the largest available sheets of copper, and confronted Rouault with these heliogravure plates, suggesting that a little touching up here and there would bring the plates up to the high level of the paintings. At this point, the obstinacy passed from Vollard to Rouault. Any artist thoughtful of his time, his energy, and the tasks in other forms he wished to undertake would happily have followed Vollard's suggestion, "finishing" the plates as an old-fashioned sculptor would finish work made by a pointing machine from his design. The heliogravure process was invented for printing, and a few clarifications of line or deepening of tone would have been satisfactory to many artists. Not to Rouault, however.

He groaned in spirit but he took back the copperplates and went to work. Almost throughout World War I and again from 1922 to 1927, the working of the plates were his major occupation. He continued his painting and he made other prints, most of them fairly simple and direct, technically, compared to the fifty-eight that became the *Miserere*. He himself thought that the heliogravure engraving on the plates was a failure and should be totally eliminated. He said later that his task would have been greatly lightened if he had simply started with the copperplates, completely unmarked. That is undoubtedly true, but it may be doubted that the effects would have been so rich. In the very act of eliminating the mechanically produced images, Rouault gave his new images a depth and black glow they might not otherwise have. Also, the heliogravure is not entirely eliminated; it adds its own distinctive character to what is, on technical grounds alone, possibly the most virtuoso and varied performance in the history of printmaking.

18

There are many ways of making an intaglio surface from which to print black ink on white paper. Rouault used most of them in the *Miserere*. It was impossible for him simply to touch up his own work. It became equally impossible for him simply to add up the various applications. Each one required a whole new treatment. Some of the plates passed through as many as fifteen separate and distinguishable versions before the artist declared himself satisfied. Thus there is a tremendous immediacy in each print, as if it were done all at a blow. At the same time there is the product of a slow and even painful accretion of labor. In the spiritual terms of Rouault's vision, it is as if a lifetime of meditation on the mysteries of faith were revealed in a flash of sudden illumination. We get, together, the flash of insight and the lifetime of thought.

The methods of intaglio (the word means literally "to cut in") are addressed to the need of the plate to be recessed where the ink is to be held for printing. Etching exposes parts of the plate to the corroding effect of acid; the needed depressions are eaten into the copper, hence the name. Aquatint is a variation on etching, whereby acid is allowed to eat through a granulated covering, thus covering whole areas, or even whole plates, with a grainy texture, which is then, very slowly and carefully and laboriously, modified by hand smoothing. Engraving attacks the copper directly with a sharp edge held in the hand of the artist and used to cut into the surface. The surface may also be marked by a roulette or a rocker, both tools for cutting textured patterns into larger areas, which areas are then modified by hand, much as with aquatint. Rouault used all these methods and used them in varying combinations.

Throughout the first period of intensive work on the *Miserere* plates, Rouault lived through World War I, with France — as at the time of his birth — menaced by the Germans. Throughout the second period, in the 1920's, he watched the postwar decline in public and private morality. These two, complementary historical processes, furnish the background against which he brought the plates into existence. The sense of agony and helplessness before these two equally appalling sequences of human behavior colored much of European intellectual life throughout the period. Philosophical nihilism was in part the product

19

of such feelings of the time. So was Dada, the fantastic movement in art and poetry that used accident and chance to express and overcome a bleak despair. On a much higher level of achievement, the Berlin theater of Berthold Brecht and Kurt Weill worked with the same spiritual materials of the time and reached related conclusions: the world was in a sorry state and one could make the most reasonable choice only between suicide and mockery.

Rouault, in the *Miserere,* offers a third alternative: sharing in the Passion of Jesus Christ, a Passion that goes on until the end of time for, although borne by God, it is made by man.

During those years of the making of the *Miserere,* Rouault endured a private, professional fate that only served to underline his reactions to the European scene in politics, in economics, in social life at all levels. Ambroise Vollard no doubt felt that he was being reasonably generous with Rouault; the dealer was clearly living up to his contract agreement and even going beyond it. During the war he made arrangements to store his vast collections of Renoirs and Cézannes and other great modern masters in a safe place in the country. He gave them in charge of Rouault and placed the painter in a rural retreat where he had leisure to work and a great collection to live with. Later Vollard made over the top floor of his own house into a studio for Rouault.

Nevertheless, Rouault felt that he was being injured by Vollard. At times, apparently, he felt that the dealer had enslaved him and that he toiled as one in the mines. Rouault had several exhibitions through the 1920's and his work began to be purchased by museums; but it must have seemed to him that Vollard was not "pushing" the work as he could so well with other artists. The fate of the *Miserere* itself illustrates that aspect of Vollard's professional style that Rouault found so irritating and frustrating that, decades later, as an old man, he would still talk for hours about the injustices he had suffered from Ambroise Vollard.

The series was finished in 1927 — not to Rouault's complete satisfaction, for an inability to be satisfied with his own work was one of the lifelong characteristics of the man. The original idea of having one hundred plates had been given up. There were to be fifty-eight. The original idea of two volumes was also given up. There would be one,

20

to be called *Miserere et Guerre*. Rouault brought this work to a conclusion, put final touches on the plates, took first impressions, or proof prints, announced himself well enough pleased, and awaited publication of the work to which he had given so much, upon which his professional reputation might at last be judged by a sustained major effort unequaled in the twentieth century.

Publication day never came while Vollard was alive.

Vollard may have felt the time was not ripe. He may have felt that Rouault needed to be better known as an artist before the considerable expenses of publication could be risked. He may very well simply not have had the money, for the ambitious *animateur* had been animating widely during the 1920's and his interest was much more in bringing into existence fine and unusual productions than it was in appealing to a mass market. Years later Rouault wrote that Vollard "had taste and a keen desire to make beautiful books without breaking any speed records, but it would have taken three centuries to bring to perfection the various works and paintings with which, in utter disregard of earthly limitations, he wished to burden the pilgrim."

The relationship with Vollard, undertaken when it seemed an unhoped-for miracle, was now a burden, a frustration, a tragedy.

And Rouault, in 1927, was no young artist waiting for his first introduction to the world. He was fifty-six and had poured most of the energies of his artistic maturity so far into what he saw as the dubious service of Ambroise Vollard. The painter carefully supervised the printing of the fifty-eight plates of the *Miserere*. Four hundred and fifty impressions of each were made. Vollard put the impressions into storage and had the copperplates canceled by scoring the surface in a grid pattern. The series achieved a kind of underground reputation. Proofs from the individual plates were circulated in Paris and captured all who saw them. The total work became one of those expectations looked forward to by those involved in any field of endeavor. The American ambassador to Paris wished to have several of the copperplates replated in gold and set into the wall of the embassy, but this was never possible.

Rouault continued his work. He did other prints, including some in color, but the truth is, none of them so expresses the agony of human existence and the redemption of that agony in Christ — or anything comparable — as forcefully as does the *Miserere*. Like other French artists of the time, he designed the costumes and sets for a ballet produced by the great impressario, Diaghilev: the ballet, *The Prodigal Son*, was set to music by the Soviet composer, Prokofiev. Painfully, slowly, Rouault's reputation grew, but it grew at a better rate abroad than it did in his beloved France. England, Germany, and the United States showed greater readiness to understand Rouault's art than did Paris.

At long last, in 1937, French recognition came on the scale the work demanded. A large exhibition of his paintings took place at the Petit-Palais as one of the "Masters of Independent Art" shown in connection with the Paris World's Fair of that year. The exhibition was a revelation to his countrymen and became one to the world. That show was the first of a continuing series of major exhibitions of his work which, eventually, was to include many world capitals and such American cities as New York, Boston, Washington, Cleveland, Chicago, Los Angeles, and San Francisco.

As this process began, two things happened. In 1939, World War II started on the Polish boundary, plunging Europe and eventually most of the world back into one large part of the agony Rouault had seen and chronicled most of his life. Also in 1939 Ambroise Vollard died and Rouault was free at last of what he had long regarded as an intolerable arrangement. There were several unfinished questions and they would be settled after the war.

The painting that the world just began to see and to appreciate as World War II moved closer was sober and luminous, in thick areas of color deliberately built up until it often had a "profile" almost like that of a high-relief sculpture. This middle period of Rouault's painting developed simultaneously with his work on the *Miserere*. The connections through subject matter and general human attitude are clear enough. There is also a technical connection, although, as the physical process of the *Miserere* makes clear, with Rouault there is no such thing as a purely technical question.

The point is that the paintings were built up in a manner very like that of the *Miserere* prints. Rouault painted and put aside, painted

22

and put aside for years. The paint achieved its almost sculptural quality not as an interesting textural device but out of the steady pursuit by the painter of a goal forever beyond him. The time during which the paintings were executed actually figures in them, just as it does in the prints. In the paintings that time is expressed, partly, through the buildup of the pigment, witness to hours of painting, meditating on Christ in the world and in men's hearts, repainting, adding, covering, adding again, looking, thinking, until the surface becomes a thick wall that is the accumulated record of years of spiritual thought inextricably combined with "painterly" thought and action.

The manner was to change again. The war ended. Rouault found himself a world celebrity in art. His paintings were prized and sought everywhere. His prices rose. Museum after museum joined in giving homage to the painter. Rouault appreciated this, but he had two things to do to keep his own record as an artist straight. Both involved litigation with the Vollard estate.

In 1948 he accomplished them both. After all those years he secured his rights to the *Miserere* and published it, presenting all at once the ultimate statement of his purpose in art and life. At this fulfillment he was seventy-seven.

The second achievement was negative, but it was the most effective blow struck in our time for the integrity of an artist and for his rights in his own work. Basing his position on the terms of his original contract with Vollard, Rouault in 1947 brought successful suit against the Vollard estate for recovery of some eight hundred paintings left in the studio provided him by the dealer. His formal plea for equity and justice had two counts. The first was simply that many of the paintings had been dispersed with no compensation for him. The second, referring to his slow methods, said that his professional reputation would inevitably be damaged by the circulation of paintings he himself regarded as unfinished. He won the suit and in 1948, in the presence of witnesses, destroyed by fire three hundred and fifteen of the paintings so recovered.

This action, the destruction of well over a million dollars in proved monetary value, was all but incomprehensible to the modern world; it bordered on blasphemy, not for the sake of the art but for the sake of all that money. If he thought about it, Rouault certainly approved his own "blasphemy," for the act, like his work and thought and life, pointed beyond the morality of money to something else. The overriding consideration for him was simply that these three hundred and fifteen paintings were not satisfactory and, given his advanced age, it was unlikely that he would have the time to bring them all to successful completion.

This is the same simple honesty with which his career began. When he was apprenticed to the stained-glass maker, Rouault used to save money for drawing materials by pocketing the carfare he was given for errands; but, so that his employer would not lose by this saving, the boy would run alongside the streetcar.

In those last years another echo of his youth returned redeemed. Before Vollard arrived on the scene, when the young Rouault family was desperate for food and clothing, friends and the clergy used to urge Rouault to paint religious pictures in the acceptable style of the nineteenth-century Academy. Churches, religious societies, and devout individuals would buy these, it was pointed out to him. No one would buy the violent work he was painting. Rouault refused. Now at last, half a century later, his standing apart from the poor taste of the officially devout ended in his recognition by the Church. When he was eighty, the French government made him a Commander of the Legion of Honor. Two years later Pope Pius XII named him Commander of the Order of St. Gregory the Great. More important, work of his in oil, in tapestry, and in stained glass was commissioned and executed for churches. The most genuinely religious art of modern times had succeeded in opening the eyes of organized religion to new religious expression of eternal values.

That expression is summed up in the fifty-eight prints of the *Miserere*. Man lives in a terrifying jungle largely of his own making, for the shadows and the perils of the jungle he finds within his own heart as well as in the outer world. But whatever is endured by man is endured also by the Son of Man, the Son of God. In the suffering of Christ we find our salvation and our purification.

Rouault died in 1958 and became the first artist in history to be given a state funeral by the government. When he died he was eighty-

24

six and, despite the burdens of age, he had kept on working to the end. In his painting for the last decades a new lightness had appeared, sometimes as glowing bouquets of flowers, sometimes as an aureole of light coming from the head of Christ, most often, however, as a luminous landscape, with or without figures, over which a rosy sky illuminated the world. Asked about this departure in his work, Rouault explained it in a sentence that speaks as well for the ultimate conclusion, the final meaning, of the *Miserere*: "I spent my life painting twilights. I ought to have the right now to paint the dawn."

Georges Rouault's
MISERERE

PLATE ONE: *Miserere mei, Deus, secundum magnam misericordiam tuam.* (Ps 51:1)

Have mercy on me, God, according to Thy great mercy.

We begin the journey — Christ's Way of the Cross, Georges Rouault's Way, to find our Way. Heaven looks down upon the patient Christ and upon the world. The face of the angel, recalling relief sculpture on ancient tombs, has the detachment of the knowledge of the good and evil of eternity. On that face is the full awareness of the horror of the Crucifixion, of the glory of the Resurrection.

The title picture represents at once all Heaven surveying the struggle of Christ for mankind and mankind's struggle against and for Christ. Above the earth are the crossed olive branches, a conventional symbol for peace, the peace "which is not of this world" but which we seek daily in our lives and which has been sought down through the ages. The angel and the olive branches place Christ in the tomb He entered for us. The flat stylized view of Heaven is the gravestone of that tomb.

Christ, in the garden, in the tomb, in the world, is at the beginning of the epic Way. His head is bowed with the weight of the sins of mankind of all time. He faces His ordeal not asking that the cup be taken away but with the full knowledge of what "not My Will but Thine" entails. He is in and of the world and the world stretches beyond Him as the wasteland. The scene is set. We have begun.

29

PLATE TWO: *Jésus honni . . .*

Jesus reviled . . .

As in a motion picture, we move in closer to the figure of Christ. Heaven is gone. Christ stands alone in the world. The wasteland of the earth begins to take on definite form, for it is the path upon which the Way of Christ must be followed step by step. The crown of thorns presses into His head. The exalted resolution of the title page has changed to fortitude against actual pain.

Two thousands years ago, as today, it is the moment of accepted agony. The impossible simplicity of the Word has been spoken and man chooses his own complexity. Christ is isolated but the shouts of the crowd are heard. He fills the world with His message and the world hears Him not, deafened by the taunts and jeers.

Deep into the plate, Rouault created this image. Christ seems to absorb into Himself all pain, all sorrow, all cruelty. We look deeper and deeper into the black lines and feel first the physical pain and then the moral pain. We think: How could they have done this? Rouault forces us to look more closely at the impossible depth of those black lines until we finally say: How can we do this? In setting forth upon this journey the Way leads to ourselves. We take the Way of Christ and find what He did for us. Along that Way we find what we do to Him.

PLATE THREE: *toujours flagellé . . .*

eternally scourged . . .

We come closer and closer to the agony of Christ, and closer, too, to the realization of our part in that agony. In the very title Rouault stresses "eternally" by not capitalizing the word. He stresses it in his technique on the plates.

In the first two prints the lines of Christ's head and body were broad and infinitely deep, and we saw the effect of agony upon His face. We move to a full-length view here and see the blows upon His body. Rouault's tools, themselves, are made symbols of the punishment inflicted on Christ because He loved mankind. The surface shows plainly the nature of those tools: the steel edge gouges into the smooth copperplate; the etcher's acid burns and eats the copper. Again and again Rouault worked the plates. He says, "On each plate, more or less felicitously, without ceasing or pausing, I worked with different tools; there is no secret about my methods. Never satisfied, I resumed each subject endlessly, sometimes in as many as twelve or fifteen successive states; I should have liked them all to be of equal quality." The variety of the violence, the intensity of the treatment — to copper and to Christ — take us progressively deeper into man's cruelty to God.

Rouault now gives us sixteen prints of man's cruelty to man, set against these first three prints in which Christ shows us how to accept suffering. We meet many people and each of them, to the degree we dare to see it, becomes each of us.

33

PLATE FOUR: *se réfugie en ton coeur, va-nu-pieds de malheur . . .*

seek refuge in your heart, poor wanderer . . .

On the Way, Christ stands alone against an empty world. We come now to man and to a man who typifies the human condition, man on the road, man in search, man the beggar. What he asks is love from one other human being. What he gets, even from a child, is a turning away, a look of indifference, a complete disinterest.

His burden is heavy, his road has no end. His emaciated arm is grotesque as if pulled out of the socket by the endlessly repeated act of asking for love in a world that refuses to see him. The wanderer and the world he wanders in have had love offered by the scourged Christ whose slope of shoulder and bend of neck shape this human figure who moves against the same empty space that is Christ's background on earth.

And the little boy, whose features we cannot discern, has already, in his short journey, been shaped by the loneliness and sorrow which is the common lot. His shoulders and back feel so soon the weight of the world and the effect of unkindness received and given. The twig is bent at a very early age and the rage at unrequited demands can be seen in the tiniest infant. We tend to idealize childhood, our own and that of our children. This child, at this moment, is not a happy one.

All of us teach children not to talk to strangers. We tell them to love everyone, too. This man has suffered many rebuffs. Our search for love is a lifelong one. We come closest to finding it when we search in our hearts our manner of giving it.

PLATE FIVE: *Solitaire, en cette vie d'embûches et de malices.*

Alone in this life of snares and malice.

"Eternally scourged," this man sinks down beneath his troubles. Forearm, bent head, and upper arm form an inescapable circle of despair, a circle repeated by the torso, the rocks, and the arm. The landscape of loneliness, which before this has been merely indicated by a line or a brush stroke, here rises up to embrace the whole man. He seems to rest his elbow on a mountain, the horizon is as high as his waist. Oppressed by the world, he confines his thoughts to the world and the terrors it presents him.

Rouault brings to mind all the great books you have read, all the heroes of literature, all the great men of the Bible. You look back to the *Iliad* and the *Odyssey,* to the *Aneid,* to the lives of the saints, the *Inferno, Pilgrim's Progress*, and back up through all the literature, good and bad, to the daily account of man's struggle against the snares and malice in the newspapers.

We all have sad tales to tell and each of us has felt at some time that ours was the saddest. "Injustice collectors" all, we fail sometimes to see the injustices we inflict. The cry of "Why?" echoes down the ages and it is easier to find the answer for other people than for ourselves. The *Miserere* should be "read" forward and backward, and quite often one at a time. At this point it is good to look back one by one and then start up again. This man seems so similar to the Christ of "eternally scourged" and "Jesus reviled." It is a measure of Rouault's achievement to look again at the difference.

PLATE SIX: *Ne sommes-nous pas forçats?*

Are we not convicts?

In this first set of five men, or aspects of man, we come to the first in an electrifying series of three plates which as an independent triptych would be one of the major works of this century and one of the great statements about man on the earth. *Miserere* is in its entirety a total complete great work of art. Individually each plate stands alone and yet each relates to every other one. Beyond that relationship you will find series and series within series. As you look at these plates again and again they grow for you as you grow with them. This is the essence of the experience of great art. Many people have understood the meaning of art for the first time when the power of "Are we not convicts?" hit them.

For we are all convicts. For the first time in this series a head is raised. With the raising of that head there comes no easy snapping of the chains of despair but the profound realization that love, too, has its chains. Whatever our state in life, whatever our stage of life we struggle against the demands made upon us. The human dilemma is between the loneliness of love sought and the implacable human bondage of love returned. Every life has endless annoying duties. One artist wrote, "My life is composed of so grotesque a series of busynesses that mailing a photograph is almost beyond me." We all, quite often, feel that way.

Rouault reminds us, in the nakedness of the figure and in its stance, that the chains of love are worn by Christ and delivered Him to torture and to death.

PLATE SEVEN: *nous croyant rois.*

we believe ourselves kings.

Rouault asks "Are we [not *you* but *we*] not convicts?" and answers "*we* believe ourselves kings." The wanderer and the man alone in the snares and malice receive our pity the first time we see them; and it takes many of us quite a while, and then usually at the more difficult times in our lives, to identify with them. Everyone has a pile of chains, from the first "no" he receives as a small child to the frustrations of old age, and most people "have a little list." When we look at the convict we immediately recognize our bonds with a sense of self-pity and a certain pride in our forbearance. And we are grateful to Rouault and admire his insight into our problems.

The half-mad king makes us laugh. We react spontaneously to the sly look of his eye, the self-conscious smile, the hunch of his shoulders, the uncertainty of the shoulder and arm. We see him as someone else and we are amused at his foolishness. The crown over such a face is the substance of humor and it is a relief to laugh after all the seriousness so far.

But as we look at the title again we realize that Rouault, almost a model of unpretentiousness, includes himself and includes all of us as well. With compassion, with sympathy, Rouault pushes us deeper into honesty and sends us back to the first plates to look again at the humility of the King of Kings.

Qui ne se grime pas?

Who does not wear a mask?

Yet in all honesty, in all charity, who can be completely honest all the time?

Babies wear no masks and they enchant us. But little children must learn to put them on, and often we must teach them. Rouault gives us the classic figure of the clown in one of his letters in which he writes of a chance encounter which occurred in 1903 when he was thirty-two: "One day I noticed how, when a beautiful day turns to evening, the first star shines out in the sky. It moved me deeply — I don't know why — and it marked the beginnings of poetry in my life. A gypsy caravan halted at the side of the road, a weary old horse nibbling stunted grasses, an old clown patching his costume — that was how it began. We all wear a spangled dress of some sort, but if someone catches us with the spangles off, as I caught that old clown, oh! the infinite pity of it! . . . I have made the mistake . . . of never allowing people to keep their spangles on . . ."

Later Rouault said: "Anyone who bases his entire art on one glance from a broken-down acrobat must be crazed with pride — or entirely humble, if that's the purpose he was made for."

"The show must go on" — and this clown will pull himself together for it. Rouault shares with us the glance he saw. No one who looks at the picture will wonder at the effect on him. The artist was forty-three when he began this series in 1914 and fifty-six in 1927 when they were printed. We see that glance in many of his paintings but nowhere is it as penetrating as we see it here.

PLATE NINE: *Il arrive parfois que la route soit belle . . .*

It happens, sometimes, that the way is
beautiful . . .

In spite of all our faults and all our troubles, life is a lovely gift.
Between the darkening sky and the mystery of the sea, a thin line of
light follows the curving horizon. On the shore the family is peaceful.
In the boats, the work goes well.

This is an ordinary day, the kind we do not notice until we look
back upon it in memory much later. It is the day Emily asks to relive
in Thornton Wilder's *Our Town*. We recall her shock that no one knew
the beauty and wonder of it in the concern for the daily duties.

Memory plays us strange tricks. We think it will be the holidays
and the great moments that will live on with us. Proust's conjuring
up the past through a little cake and a cup of tea has been experienced
by all of us, each in a special way. This is really the day we all strive
for, the peace we think we seek, this day when the work progresses and
the family grows in love. Rouault helps us feel the rhythm of life
and lets us rest before we go on.

As we go on in life we often remember this print at unexpected
times when we realize with a slight surprise that "the way is beautiful."

PLATE TEN: *au vieux faubourg des Longues Peines.*

in the old district of Long-Suffering.

The series was begun at the start of World War I. Rouault was in his forties. Life may begin at forty, and in some ways it does, for then many of us begin to sense the rhythm of the ups and downs. Call it reliance on Divine Providence, call it, as Renoir did, "an aversion to making decisions: the 'cork,' you remember . . . ," he said (speaking to his son, Jean, alluding to his favorite theory). "You go along with the current. . . . Those who want to go against it are either lunatics or conceited; or what is worse 'destroyers.' You swing the tiller over to the right or left from time to time, but always in the direction of the current." By forty, most of us realize we don't control the course and most of us have lived in the Old District of Long-Suffering one way or another.

The husband is not here but we know him from the five men we have seen in the preceding plate, and from the happy family group. The baby clutches the mother. The mother's head is bowed as Christ's was bowed and she takes comfort as she gives comfort. The little girl stands close but just a bit apart. She is old in her patience, old in her quietness.

Rouault was born in just such an old district of Long-Suffering. He began the series when all France seemed to belong to that District. It is the address of the human race.

Demain sera beau, disait lenauf ragé . . .

Tomorrow will be beautiful, said the shipwrecked man . . .

In a poem, Rouault adds: " — before he disappeared beneath the sullen horizon."

The shipwrecked man, who has struggled to this island, stands on quicksand, and reaches to grasp an uprooted tree. In the world of catastrophes to be met, as we go on to others, Rouault calls our attention to our endless capacity for hope in adversity and to our endless capacity for self-delusion.

In the Old District of Long-Suffering there seems to be a total acceptance of calamity. Beside that acceptance and beside the love that grows as we accept stands the straight, strong form of the tree. Here in the wild storm, in man's refusal to accept reality, that same tree is pulled up from the ground and swings wildly in the wind.

We all have moments when hardship follows hardship, when we grasp at anything to save us. We all hope "tomorrow will be beautiful." The time-payment system is based on that hope. The rearing and training of children looks to tomorrow. "Next payday," "next week," "next year" are magic words we base our lives on, and in looking back toward the past and forward to the future we lose the present.

PLATE TWELVE: *Le dur métier de vivre...*

It is hard to live...

The man grows older. He is less bent but more resigned to the business of life. He does not seek as much as the wanderer, is not as shocked by the snares and malice; he does not strain as the convict nor is he fatuous as the king, woebegone as the clown, as desperate as the shipwrecked man.

He accepts the hardships of life, too tired to rebel against them, too worn for pride, too wise for hope. There is dignity in his acceptance and there is nobility in his strength. He pauses as we paused before for a little time when the way was beautiful. The way is not beautiful now but neither is it the Old District of Long-Suffering. It is in between and we know he will be happy again and he will be unhappier again.

We often grow tired on the way. Christ fell three times. Three times he paused and three times he rose and went on. Many are the times we feel it is hard to live. For many of us the hard times are at the beginning of the day and at the end of it. In between we often muddle through.

"I can't, any more . . ." rings through our lives or sometimes just "I can't." But life goes on. It is only in fiction and in the theater that it stops. Life is particularly hard as long as we pause to find how hard it is.

PLATE THIRTEEN: *il serait si doux d'aimer.*

it would be so sweet to love.

We have seen five men, two families, two more men. And now we begin a series of five women. As with all of them — as with the first three of Christ — they are all of us: as we are and as we would like to be.

The mother and child are alone and are together. The child, in spite of her old-young face, in spite of her position when we met her before, completely rests in her mother's love, absorbed with the gift, we like to think, of childhood, in the immediacy of the moment.

Rouault, in the heartbreaking subjunctive of the title, shows us the mother, wary, with the knowledge of the past and the menace of the future. She is tense; her mouth is stern. She looks down upon her child with love, with fear, with compassion. Her hand does not press her daughter to her. It points out to the world. This mother already knows the complexity of discipline, the endless demands of mundane affairs and the ever growing limits to her protection.

Parents explore daily how sweet it *would* be to love and to be loved. Daily they learn the intricacies of stewardship, the mysteries of justice, the otherness of their children, the limits of their ability to cope with their awesome responsibilities. Besieged on all sides with advice from "experts," harrassed by constant demands upon them, parents grow in love as they learn what they do not know. We saw the head of this home in Plate Six. Here is the heart of the home. The bend of her head and her patience bring us back again to Christ.

PLATE FOURTEEN: *Fille dite de joie.*

They call her daughter of joy.

Soon after 1900 Rouault began a series of paintings which savagely attack the evils of society. He had been doing academic paintings of traditional sacred images. He had studied great painters and had done many sketches reminiscent of their work. Suddenly, tremendously influenced by his meeting with Léon Bloy and his reading of Bloy's book, *The Woman Who Was Poor,* he began to paint the world he saw around him. Bloy was shocked at these paintings and wrote to him: "Naturally I saw your one and only, sempiternal canvas, forever the same slut or the same clown, with this single lamentable difference that, each time, the scum seems to increase. . . ." Bloy never became reconciled with Rouault's fierce indictments of the society that Bloy himself castigated in his prose. Raissa Maritain writes: "How many times in the following years did we not see Rouault at Bloy's house, standing and leaning against the wall, with a slight smile on his closed lips, his gaze far off, his face apparently impassive but with a pallor that increased when the question of modern painting was broached."

To the horror of many, Rouault kept on, and his paintings of judges, prostitutes, and the poor clowns stand as some of the most horrifying statements of the cruelty of man. "They call her daughter of joy" is far from the paintings of that era. Rouault's charity touches all the degrees of human prostitution, based as it is in the tragic desire to purchase and possess in a moment what cannot be bought but must be built and built slowly over years of trouble shared and sorrow surmounted. The actual woman of the streets is here seen as the victim of social forces totally beyond her comprehension or even her awareness of their existence.

PLATE FIFTEEN: *En bouche qui fut fraîche, goût de fiel.*

On lips that were fresh, the taste of gall.

In that letter in 1907 about the early paintings, Léon Bloy went on: "I have two things to say to you today, after which you will be no more to me than a friendly carcass. First: you are attracted exclusively by the ugly, your head is swimming with hideous sights. Second: if you were a man of prayer and obedience, if you were a thanks-giver, you would be incapable of painting these horrible canvasses. A Rouault capable of depth would feel slightly terror-stricken."

It was precisely because of his depth, precisely that he was so terror-stricken that Rouault lashed out with such paintings. He has been called the painter of original sin. In this print we come to an even more sympathetic, even more charitable understanding of the women he, in the earlier years, painted with such fury.

This girl has a much more intelligent face, indicating a higher capacity for suffering, and a more advanced form of prostitution. Suffering here springs from the precise knowledge of what is being sold and at what a pitiful price. The business of selling oneself is only touched upon but extends out from the effect on her face. The mind can be sold, and is. God-given talent, in so many directions, can be sold and is. The soul, itself, can have its price.

Dame du Haut-Quartier croit prendre pour le Ciel place réservée.

The well-bred lady thinks she has a reserved seat in Heaven.

The way to come to know Rouault, as to come to know any artist, is to look at his work again and again, day after day. Paintings, sculpture, and prints in our homes grow for us as we grow and when we visit and revisit our museums, there too our friends show us new aspects of life. Everything we come to know about an artist, everything we come to know about life, we bring to his art, and our affection grows.

Rouault shows a strong and deep religious development up through the years from the first violent expressions against a corrupt society in his youth, through the maturing of his middle years to the serene sunsets of his old age. At first the well-bred lady seems to take us back to the severity of his youth. But there is a great difference.

The difference is in the growth in compassion. We have seen in the two prints before this one the immense sympathy Rouault evokes. At first glance here, we laugh as we laughed at the king, but Rouault goes beneath the pretensions of the society woman. She, too, a convict of her state in life, wears a mask of self-satisfaction, of self-righteousness, of propriety. The effort to keep the mask intact has worn a deep, straight, sad line beside her mouth, has bowed her shoulders, has set her jaw. We recall the parable of the publican and the sinner, we study the unhappiness beneath the pride, and we search ourselves for our own presumptions.

Once again we return to study the humility of Christ.

PLATE SEVENTEEN: *Femme affranchie, à quatorze heures, chante midi.*

Emancipated woman, at two o'clock, cries noon.

In other words, she doesn't know the time of day.

Like the mothers of children, emancipated women get advice from everyone and they receive a good deal of abuse. The role of women has concerned us all since World War I and for no woman — as perhaps for no woman before "emancipation" — has there been a satisfactory solution. Those who are not free from the traditional "burdens" of woman, free of childbearing, child-rearing, the demands of a household, free to seek their own pleasures, find they are accused of "retreating into fecundity" and are not fulfilling the hopes of the women that pioneered for them. The business woman is accused of not being a woman, but finds she has not attained the privileges of a man. The woman, who is not or who is no longer imprisoned in the home but who does not go into business, is ridiculed for her clubwork and is attacked from both sides in her pursuit of leisure.

Rouault, at the beginning of the emancipation fight, shows its price. The emptiness of her life is revealed in the bewildered look, the tortured eyes, the social smile. She wears the mask of gaiety, and the pert little hat mocks her eyes in her pursuit of "fun." Again, as in the well-bred lady and in the king, Rouault denies the joke as we stare into those eyes. The issue is not fun or fecundity, profession or motherhood, or a combination of all the proposed solutions. For women, as for men, there is no easy formula for a happy life.

61

PLATE EIGHTEEN: *Le condamné s'en est allé . . .*

The condemned man went away . . .

Again and again Rouault painted utter loneliness, deep and hopeless tragedy. This man — condemned to live? condemned to die? — is abandoned by all and he quietly goes, or is taken away.

In 1907 Rouault began a series of *Judges* and *Tribunals*. For over a year he had attended trials at the Tribunal de la Seine at the invitation of a friend who was a deputy public prosecutor. His paintings of judges are perhaps the most disturbing he achieved. He said, "The reason I gave my judges such woeful faces was doubtless that I expressed the anguish I myself feel when I see one human obliged to judge another. . . . For nothing in the world would I accept the position of judge!"

In his painting *Condemned Man* of 1907, now in a private collection in Switzerland, Rouault did a portrait of a man he saw sentenced in court. The man is flanked by two judges. All three are alone, all three are terrifying. In this print, Rouault evokes pity for the man who has been judged and pity for the man who judged him.

This man accepts his sentence. It is well, here, to go back slowly over all the plates, viewing again all these people, looking at our concern for ourselves, and looking back to the model of Christ. We think how like Christ this man accepts. But there is a looking inward, a self-absorption, a self-concern that is far from what we see in Rouault's portraits of Christ. Each time we study the faces of the people and again the face of Christ, we wonder at Rouault's ability to portray the difference between God and man.

63

PLATE NINETEEN: *son avocat, en phrases creuses, clame sa totale inconscience . . .*

his lawyer, in empty phrases, proclaims his total ignorance . . .

There are many things to watch as we take this journey along the path of the *Miserere*. Rouault gave these titles to the prints and often, as here, he stresses the universality of the subject, the continuing recurrence of an event by not capitalizing the first word in a phrase and by not putting a period at the end. This was not the first lawyer to turn his back after a client was sentenced, nor will he be the last.

Again we are reminded of the early paintings, of Rouault's rage. Again we are about to laugh as we started to laugh at the king and the well-bred lady. We look at the lawyer at first with the eyes of the condemned man. Rouault, like all of us, found Christ's admonition "Love thy neighbor" harder to follow with some people, with some types, than with others. Since his own initial reaction was like ours, something of it remains in the line of the lawyer's mouth. But Rouault has been teaching us to look as we move along. We have seen a head raised like this before, the head of the convict in Plate Six. We turn back to look. There was strength, here is weakness. We have seen those shoulders on the king, on the well-bred lady. Finally we come to the pity and compassion Rouault is leading us to. Finally we come to think of the times when, in empty phrases, we have tried to shed our involvement.

65

sous un Jésus encroix oublié là.

under a Jesus forgotten on a cross.

All of these people, all the men, all the women, all of humanity from the beginning of time to the end of time are caught up and seen in the light of "under (again lower case) a Jesus forgotten on the cross," forgotten two thousand years ago, forgotten today, and forgotten tomorrow. Jesus hangs upon the cross, deep in the suffering and loneliness of the Passion, above the unheeding world.

In this series it is as if Rouault gives us just as much as we are able to comprehend, then a little more. He sends us back and forth from print to print, then sweeps us up to the impossible model of Christ before we are able to go on. He showed us more and more of Christ in each of the first three prints. He showed us ourselves and our fellow men in the prints preceding the present one. As it takes a lifetime to know the *Miserere,* how much longer does it take to know Christ and to know ourselves, to find a way with others!

By now, as we retrace our way again and again, the rhythm of Rouault's vision, the rhythm of life becomes more and more apparent. We pause here, we refresh ourselves, we contemplate. We turn back to the beginning, we see the intervening plates with new compassion, with new horror. We see this present title with new realization of Christ's message of charity, with new comprehension of how His message has fallen on deaf ears. We have a heightened view of how life could be, we have a deeper sense of how it is.

"Il a été maltraité et opprimé et il n'a pas ouvert la bouche." (Is 53:7)

"He has been maltreated and oppressed and he has not opened his mouth."

Rouault has often been called a hermit, a recluse, a mystic. All those words imply silence, a man who seldom spoke. Legends quickly attach themselves to artists, even in their own lifetimes. Already Rouault is characterized in short accounts as moody, secretive, fanatical. He is quoted as having said, "I do not want to be known."

The truth is that Rouault apparently had as much trouble keeping his mouth shut as the rest of us do. The list of his published books is a long one; he published many poems; and he wrote long letters to his friends. André Girard wrote: "He spoke so abundantly that he rarely left time for an answer. And he completed these talks by letters, written very often just after he left me." His close friend, André Suarès, followed the same practice as Rouault. They met frequently and used to complete their conversations by letters. They have left thousands of letters — now to be published — which are a mixture of verses, philosophical essays, stories about the neighbors, technical data — the "trivial next to the divine."

It should be clear that no recluse ever knew his fellowman in the way Rouault is showing us he did in this series. Rouault was a recluse from the organized art world. He had to be protected by his devoted family and friends, he had to protect himself to find time to do the work he wanted to do. Even in the exerpts from his conversations and writings we catch the irony, the humor, the gentleness, and the enjoyment of a strong-minded man having a good time with his friends. He attacked the nonsense of the art world whenever he had a chance. It was because he found it so easy to open his mouth that he could create this impossible ideal.

PLATE TWENTY-TWO: *En tant d'ordres divers, le beau métier d'ensemencer une terre hostile.*

In so many different ways, the beautiful calling of sowing a hostile earth.

From the vision of Jesus forgotten on the cross, silent in the face of insult and injury, Rouault turns again to man's daily life on earth, where, if anywhere, salvation made possible by the Crucified, must be worked out by every man.

"What I like about peasants," Rouault once wrote, "is the slowness with which they move and the hardness of their lives." His liking for farmers is far from the conventional admiration of life in the country long held by painters and poets and now shared by most of us as we find ourselves more and more inescapably in the city. Rouault is not talking about the sunsets or the gentle swell of meadows or the splintering of light through leaves. He knows the farmer's life to be a hard one — "sowing a hostile earth" — and sees that it is precisely in the hardships and hard work that "in so many different ways" life on the land is beautiful.

The hardness and the slowness are carved into every line of this sower. His hand outstretched in the timeless act of dropping seed into the furrowed earth seems also to be outstretched in a humble prayer for the harvest. His head is bowed to the earth, like those of oxen plowing; the sections of his shoulders, back, and neck, heavily outlined in black, might almost be fieldstones, those firmly embedded rocks the farmer must move, with great labor, just to go on with his work.

On the land or in the town, man must sow the "hostile earth," protect and cherish whatever it yields.

Lonely Street.

For the man working on the land, the world was dark more than it was light. The darkness gave way in three places: along his arm, on his brow, and, more than anywhere, on the face of his house in the distance. Against that comforting light of home, Rouault now contrasts the all too available light in the city, the garish light that blinds without illumination and without warmth. In the city of man, along the street of the lonely ones, the solitaries, there is more light than there was in the whole countryside. And there is more darkness. The light, gleaming on the pocked fronts of buildings, has the deadness of white bones, the darkness the deep shadow of approaching despair.

In this and the preceding plates, Rouault is not accepting the simple-minded comparison that finds the rural life good, the urban life bad. Working the earth and drifting along Lonely Street are more states of mind, of heart, than they are geographical locations. The sower of fruitful seed in however hostile earth, and the lost figure in the nightmare of the city — both exist in the human heart.

At first the street looks empty. It isn't. Along the left side, past the gaping doorway of shadow, a human figure may be seen; nearby is another. Each is alone. In the view of the sower, the man, head bent, shoulders scored with labor, nevertheless loomed across the landscape, dominating nature through his own dedication. Here in the city, built by man, man nevertheless diminishes to a detail in the scene, one that must be sought out in the shadows to be found at all.

Rouault rarely uses perspective, that classical device, in this drama of the heart of man. Here he does. The lines of the street sweep toward their meeting and sweep all in the city along with them. They meet at the center of a great X formed by curbs and roof lines. They meet in a looming tower of darkness. They meet at what classical drafts-manship has always called "the vanishing point."

"Hiver lèpre de la terre."

"Winter, earth's leper."

On the land or in the town, winter is the dead time. This fugitive figure, slinking across the earth, reveals a new and chilling use of stark light. Striding against a sky filled with dark, the winter spirit represented in this figure glistens in white on its head, along its arm, its body, its purposeful legs; and the white is the white of the ancient disease, leprosy, which began the dissolution of the body while the person still lived, which turned the body silvery white in the patches where it showed, which struck terror into the hearts of man, against which, for so many centuries, there was no cure. Leprosy was the disease of the eastern Mediterranean, and therefore one of the few illnesses mentioned in the New Testament. In that medieval France that Rouault so often recalls, the leper went about with bell or rattle to warn the healthy. The leper was condemned, for the sake of society, to wander the earth as man himself is condemned to wander in time.

Here the stricken wanderer takes his way, bearing his illness like a heavy shadow shaped to his bent head, to his back.

Winter is also a time of life and not necessarily the end of life, although it can be. It is a time when all efforts come to naught, when effort itself seems not worth making. The snow of difficulty and obstacle piles higher and becomes that snow of the body that with terror the medieval leper saw upon his skin. The dead time spreads its chill silently into the fiber of the soul through whatever works we take up and put down. Cold and ill, we wander like the leper, hoping only to avoid infecting those we meet with the fatal sickness of despair.

*Jean-François jamais ne chante
alleluia . . .*

Jean-François never sings
alleluia . . .

There is a spiritual winter not only in the lives of men but also in the life of a human society. Rouault, like his prophetic teacher, Léon Bloy, deeply believed that such a winter had settled in over Europe with the coming of an industrial civilization in the nineteenth century. Here is the victim of that new kind of society, the exploited worker upon whose backbreaking toil all the new wealth was built. The lines of labor are cut into the face. Life is endured; it is never celebrated.

As Rouault entered upon the long meditation that was to become the *Miserere,* the Christian churches were just beginning to realize that the new class, the "proletariat," had been lost to Christianity. Popes, beginning with Leo XIII, pointed out the disaster that had befallen the Faith; for generation after generation of the laboring poor, religion was a meaningless series of observances, sometimes followed, sometimes ignored, but a thing with no relevance to the lives of the poor in the city of man. Christianity, the religion of the poor, was separated from the poor. It would be decades, perhaps centuries, before the message of Christ would again be received as words of hope to the despairing. "The poor have the Gospel preached to them" was a long way away, in the past or in the future.

In this humble, tragic figure, Rouault painfully confronts us with the reality of the "working class" in the "post-Christian" era. The sorrow and the wound of the separation do not come from the "loss" to the Church, but in the loss of celebration as a part of life. In the joyless world of commercial society, Jean-François has neither the strength nor the occasion to sing "Alleluia."

77

PLATE TWENTY-SIX: *au pays de la soif et de la peur.*

in the land of thirst and fear.

Jean-François represents a particular problem of a particular moment in time, and we have not solved that problem yet, although a measure of social justice has been obtained. But the feeling of Jean-François, hopelessly cut off from the world he must live in, isolated and adrift, is universal, not of one time, one place. It is the situation of man on earth. Rouault here widens our vision from the tragic figure of an individual worker to the strange landscape of life.

It is a strange landscape, too, such as might be seen in a dream, or in a quietly terrifying nightmare. The frail boat drifts on the water. There is no sail, there is no wind. One sits, lost in brooding. One stands, holding to the mast — in vain. If the boat is becalmed, no change of the rigging will raise the wind. If the boat moves, it moves from forces invisible, for the surface of the water is dead too, unmoving, unrippled, producing a perfect mirror image of the strange building on the shore.

The strange building is unlike anything in European shelters or monuments, somewhat suggestive of Islam, which was a mystery and a terror to Christian Europe. The strange tree, on the left, looks almost like some malignant flower grown to monstrous size. In the background, strange plants seem to grow in a land otherwise a desert. On the horizon the light lingers but will be gone soon.

We are in "the land of thirst and fear."

We are in the strange country of life on earth.

PLATE TWENTY-SEVEN: *"Sunt lacrymae rerum . . ."*
(Virgil, *Aeneid I*)

"There are tears in things . . ."

Virgil, long ago, wrote of such a country. Through it wandered Orpheus, the singer, searching for his wife, Euridyce, who was dead. He came to the country of the dead and bargained for her release and won it and led her back toward the living, and lost her at the last turning of the stair. Twice bereaved, Orpheus went forward to his own death, having made music out of sorrow but not, on that account, having conquered sorrow or triumphed over death.

The sweet song of Orpheus is sung in the curves of this composition. Kneeling in sorrow, Orpheus raises his head to the final knowledge of death. His body curves and the curve is heightened in his cloak, sweeping out and down from shoulder to knee. The vertical curve of Orpheus's body is balanced against the curve of the horizon, the meeting of dark earth and light sky at the edge of the world, along which Orpheus voyaged, once to find the Golden Fleece, once to find the dead Euridyce. The magic lyre hangs at his side, silent. No music now will console the musician nor charm his love again to life.

The tilt of the face toward the light and the thrust upward of the neck, we have seen before. They are the posture of the man in Plate Six, "Are we not convicts?" The bringer of music to mankind, one of the sweetest conceptions of the ancient, pre-Christian world, must, like the humblest wanderer in the world, bare his throat to the knife the world has always ready for the cut.

In this graceful resignation we see the highest wisdom of the ancient world. We live in death's dominion and must accept its doom.

"Celui qui croit en moi, fût-il mort, vivra." (Jn 11:25)

"He who believes in Me, though he be dead, shall live."

The words of the Gospel bring the believer beyond the graceful resignation of Orpheus and Virgil. Death is not the end of all things but the beginning of life.

We descend into the house of the dead. This is not the mythical kingdom of the dead of Orpheus, but the reality of the charnel house, a place of terror for mankind confronted with the dead and the thought that he, too, must die. This place is not just beyond the edge of the world. It is within our cities, upon the countryside. The dead are placed there. The low curve of the ceiling is pressed down with the weight of earth. The darkness of the wall deepens into total night in the corners. Arranged in rows upon shelves, the skulls of the dead comprise a grisly congregation for the Gospel words.

Yet those words shall set them free. The shelves converge upon the door of the tomb, to which also steps rise up from the floor. On the top step rests one more skull and above that skull towers the sign of the cross, marked upon the inner side of the tomb.

In the world of Virgil, death upon the cross was worse than that death every man journeyed toward. This was not so much because of the pain as because of the total shame of such a death. The crucified was an outcast, condemned by his society, sent broken into death. But the Gospel of redemption has gloried in that ancient mark of shame. What was broken on the Cross was death's dominion itself.

The door of the tomb is marked with the Cross and the door opens outward.

PLATE TWENTY-NINE: *Chantez Matines, le jour renaît.*

Sing Matins, day is reborn.

The door of the tomb does open. The gloom of the night still hovers, no more a menace, in the corners of this plate, but, below, the sky has lightened and its brightening depths may be measured by the soaring, coasting passage of a single bird. Between this brightening sky and the vanishing blackness above, the pure white sun — like the sun that is the Risen Christ — ascends in glory. Its rays reveal an earth that is no longer hard to sow. The earth now flows gently like the swell of the ocean wave. All things are redeemed in Christ, the earth as well as the men who live upon it. The rich flowing lines of the earth are heavier echoes of the brush strokes across the brightening sky. Christ rises; heaven and earth rejoice and sing the song of morning.

Rouault has taken us through the tragic destiny of life on earth, has shown us the warped fate that man is all too prone to make for himself, has shown us, too, the noblest expression of Mediterranean paganism in its efforts to come to terms with dreadful realities. The artist has now led us to the Christian life that comes from death.

"Though he be dead, he shall live." Christian insistence on life as the result of death becomes the artist's theme, insistently stated, in the last few plates of the *Miserere* — the first half of the series. The pace quickens as the eye is liberated from the close gloom of the house of the dead to the wide sweep of the world redeemed.

PLATE THIRTY: *"Nous . . . c'est en sa mort que nous avons été baptisés."* (Rom 6:3)

"We . . . it is in His death that we have been baptized."

The explanation is St. Paul's. Rouault illustrates it here, with the straight figure of the Baptist, the submissive Christ, the disciples at prayer, the hovering Spirit in the form of a dove, all against the infinite curve of the horizon.

Contrast to the despair of Orpheus is present in every line. The body of Christ echoes the grace of Orpheus. The light along the edge of the world is the same background we saw behind the singer. The differences are many. They are summed up in the attitude of the head. Orpheus threw back his head in final, despairing acceptance of tragic fate. Christ bows His head, beneath the presence of the Spirit, beneath the hand of the Precursor, beneath the flow of life-giving water.

There is contrast, too, between the Baptist and the Savior. John the Baptist was the last of the Old Testament prophets, and a martyr. In a special way, it is in *his* death that we are baptized, as well as in Christ's. Here he stands, not a reed shaken by the wind, but a sturdy pillar upon which the salvation of man will be built.

The cleansing waters of baptism are the waters of salvation and they are like that dawn for which we sing Matins. The night is over. The voyagers in the land of thirst and fear have found saving water to drink.

The complete calm of sky, earth, and water testifies to the new life for mankind, preached by John, sealed for us by Jesus in His blood.

PLATE THIRTY-ONE: *"Aimez-vous les uns les autres."*
(Jn 13:34)

"Love one another."

Rouault passes without pause from the moment of Christ's baptism to the moment of His death on the cross and to His message of salvation.

The Crucifixion was one of the most brutal and agonizing events in human history, a history that has been all too talented in brutality and agony. Yet here Rouault presents that event in the same calm terms as the Baptism of Christ in the preceding plate. The gentle grace of the lines of Christ's body is repeated in the figures around the cross. The curves of the woman who kneels on the left and of those who mourn on the right are repeated in the graceful hill that forms the only background.

The cross itself seems a conventional arrangement of the vertical and the horizontal, against which Christ stands, arms outstretched as if making a demonstration rather than dying a death.

It is a demonstration: upon the text from St. John. Christ on the cross instructs those who mourn Him to love one another. The Way of the Cross is not a private devotion closing out all the world from a private dialogue between Christ and His disciple. Rather, the disciple is commanded to love those he meets upon the way, his brothers in religion and his brothers in our common humanity. The Christian's love of Christ must begin in and must ever return to the love of man; and not only mankind in general, but each individual man encountered in life.

PLATE THIRTY-TWO: *Seigneur, c'est vous, je vous reconnais.*

Lord, it is You, I know You.

It is the risen Christ, the deep black lines of His features carrying the experience of the death on the cross and the obscurity of three days in the tomb, the rays of the nimbus reflecting the glory of His Resurrection.

It is a disciple in the moment of recognition. There were many such moments after the Resurrection and all are distinguished in the Gospel accounts by the restrained understatement that Rouault is guided by. The disciples are fishing and see Him on the beach, calmly preparing food for them to break their fast. Two of the group walk to Emmaus and are joined by a Stranger, whom they recognize in the breaking of the bread. There is no thunder and lightning, no drama. There is only the quiet, ordinary course of human events, a meeting between humans, often at a meal, a gesture of helpfulness, and then the sudden recognition: "It is the Lord!"

The hand of the disciple reaches out to Christ; the hand of Christ responds. The recognition is mutual. In old Christian legends, told for centuries in Rouault's France, the believer meets a Stranger on the road, helps Him, and the Stranger turns out to be Christ.

In the life enjoined by the Gospels, in the ordinary, unremarkable, day-by-day encounters of such a life, the Stranger on the road is always Christ.

PLATE THIRTY-THREE: *et Véronique au tendre lin passe encore sur le chemin . . .*

and Veronica, with her gentle cloth, still passes on the way . . .

The first half of Rouault's *Miserere* series concludes with Veronica's veil, a relic of one of the most thoughtful legends from the Ages of Faith. In those ages, when even the derivation of words was based on religious speculation rather than on science or recorded history, it was said that Veronica, who wiped Christ's face on the way to Calvary, got her name from two Latin words, *vera icon,* or "true image." For, in the legend, when Christ passed on toward His death, that woman of Jerusalem found on her cloth the imprinted image, in blood and sweat, of the face of the Savior.

In this picture, Rouault suggests such a printing. The square of cloth serves as a frame. The image is flattened out somewhat; the crown of thorns does not encircle the head but is pressed out to either side; the eyes are closed or sightless; there are smudges, as of blood.

It is the true image, simple in suffering, accepting suffering, and accepting, too, the spontaneous offer of comfort from the woman of Jerusalem. The nature of printing is to make new originals from an already existing original. This print of the face of Jesus appears on Veronica's cloth as the true image of the Lord. The truth of the image derives from the love with which the cloth was pressed to the suffering face.

Miserere, man's cry for mercy, finds its answer in man's own love for those he encounters along the way. Man becomes the true image of Christ only in mercy shown and suffering comforted.

GUERRE

PLATE THIRTY-FOUR: *"Les ruines elles-mêmes ont péri."*
(Lucian, *Pharcale IX,* 969)

"Even the ruins have been destroyed."

The title page of the second half of the series repeats the arrangement of the first. Again there is a frame all around. Again there is a face above and one below, but now they are changed. At the beginning a carved angel, as from a graveyard, hovered above; below, Christ entered upon His Passion. Now Christ is above, once more in the "true image" imprinted upon Veronica's veil, with the nimbus of glory shining out in all directions. Below is the grim figure of Death within the arch. Grimacing Death wears a soldier's helmet and at the top of the page the title announces the new subject: War.

The title, the image of Christ, the image of Death, taken together, remind us of Veronica, who, as Christ stumbled toward His death, offered a cloth. In the first of the World Wars, during which Rouault did most of the initial work on the *Miserere,* mankind revealed a new thing to do for the stranger on the road: shoot him! And blow up the road.

PLATE THIRTY-FIVE: *Jésus sera en agonie jusqu'à la fin du monde . . ." (Pascal, Pensées)*

"Jesus will be in agony until the end of the world. . . ."

Here is the Stranger on the road and what we have done with Him.

Jesus was crucified not primarily by the Roman colonial government or the clerical conspirators of the synagogue, but by the sins of all mankind through all history. Much theological thought has been devoted to elaborating the doctrine of the "just war," a notion based on the simple truth that much theological activity has always been financed by warriors, but from time to time in Christian history an anguished Christian voice has cried out to theologians and to warriors to remind them of what they are doing: they are killing people. And to remind them that the first person to be killed in any war is Christ, killed once more.

Such a voice is Rouault's throughout this second part of the *Miserere*.

Among the sins of mankind responsible for nailing Jesus to the cross, war is particularly serious. Christ's word for His crucifiers, "They know not what they do," applies to most of the people who make wars, though not, for the most part, to those who fight them. The war-maker fancies himself variously to be extending the boundaries of empire, to be fulfilling his Manifest Destiny, to be acquiring living space for his people, to be building up industry, or merely to be moving colored pins on a map. The first thing he is doing is killing people.

And here is the true image of the Person who is, first, last and always the One to be killed. The lacerated, hung-up body of Christ is also suffering mankind in mankind's wars.

Ce sera la dernière, petit père!

This will be the last time, dear father!

Among the earliest print series in Europe were those on the "Dance of Death," in which Death, characterized as a skeleton, or as an animated corpse, the flesh hanging from the bones like rags, danced his way through all the ranks of society, taking here a prince, there a beggar, now a bishop, now a child at play. The theme may have originated in late medieval morality plays, teaching the essential lesson that death comes to all men. But in the hands of the first printmen, the theme revealed a savage irony traceable to the fourteenth-century experience of the Plague in Europe which swept across the continent to vanish and reappear and take its dreadful toll in all countries.

In our time science has put an end to the plague and science has been used, also, to perfect the man-made plague of modern war. Deprived of the plague dropping down among us, we loose a Black Death of our own from the skies. To depict our invented plague, Rouault revives the language of the early woodcut artists.

He uses their irony, too. The soldier making his confession repeats the penitential promise, so often on our lips a mere formula of words: to sin no more: this will be the last time. This will indeed be the last time. Grinning death rattles his bones across the bleak landscape of hatred to make the promise good.

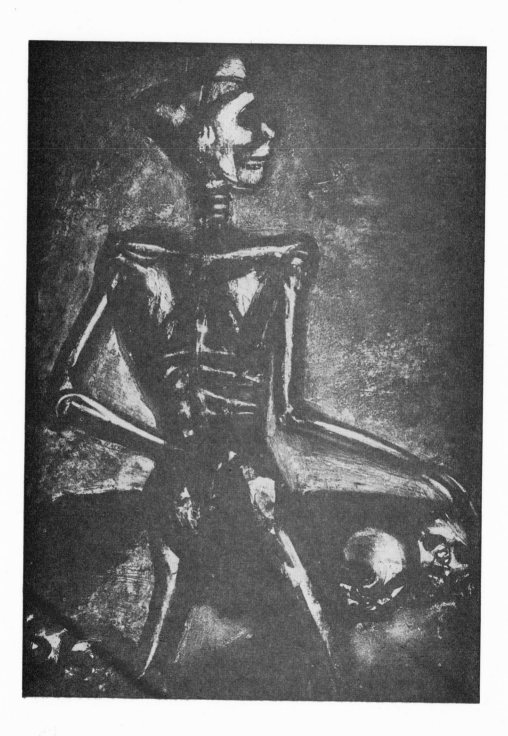

"Homo homini lupus." (Plautus, *Asinaria,* II, 4, 88)

"Man is wolf to man."

Death in a soldier's cap strides across the landscape of hatred, the country of war. In posture and position, the skeleton figure recalls another walker on the land, the sower in Plate Twenty-Two, "The beautiful calling of sowing a hostile earth." Here it is the sower himself who makes the earth hostile. Here, around the moving bones of the sower of death, we see the crop begin to rise, the skulls of the dead.

In the face of death there is a new quality, different from the vindictive delight of the death's-head in early woodcuts. The head, in fact, is not a pure skull. It is halfway between fleshed face and picked-clean skull. The nose relates the figure to the still living. But the eyes have gone. The combination of those empty sockets — black holes — and the fixed grin contains the truth: death has gone mad and wanders he knows not where over the earth.

Out from the figure, along the edge of the earth, spreads the inky black shadow. The earth is darker than the sky on a moonless night. The crop of skulls begins to grow against that jet-black earth.

The sky, too, however, is affected by its witness of the grisly events below. Etchings and aquatints are made by letting acid eat its way into copper. The sky is textured by such action: heaven itself is affected by the acid of man's hatred for man.

Like the Plague, that other ancient menace, the wolf, has been tamed and man himself has taken up the task of hunting man for prey.

Chinois inventa, dit-on, la poudre à canon, nous en fit don.

The Chinese, they say, invented gunpowder, made us a gift of it.

The Sage of the East has been a stock figure in the European imagination ever since modern Europe first made contact with the Orient. One part of European imaginings, still to be found in Europe and America, is the notion that the ancient Chinese civilization has arrived at solutions to the problems of humanity which are still unknown in the West. Westerners have traveled to the East to master the athletic arts of Yoga and the poetic arts of Zen Buddhism.

Rouault adds to the tradition and presents his own Chinese scholar, dressed in a version of the robes and headpiece of scholarship in the East. He sits bemused in his study, bemused and perhaps shocked. That he has cause for shock is clear in the title the artist has given the picture. What for the Chinese before Marco Polo was a plaything to delight the eye and the ear became for the Europeans after Marco Polo a weapon of fearful power. The Oriental, in Rouault's vision, cannot understand how a thing of beauty can be put to such inhuman use. The European would be as hard put to grasp how such a source of power could be wasted on firework festivals.

The Chinese scholar represents not so much the attitude of the East as the attitude of anyone given over to the life of the mind when confronted with the appalling waste of war. From the coolness of the study, it is impossible to understand that men would choose such a way of life.

Nous sommes fous.

We are mad.

Death, stalking over Europe in 1914 and over the whole world ever since, is mad. But he is mad because his masters are mad and have passed their madness on to him. In the twentieth century the masters are all the people; even the most extreme dictatorships go through the motions of obtaining their legitimacy from the people. Here, confronted by war, are two of the masters. Mad.

Rouault presents them so that they seem almost to be balloons, blown up to enormous size, but empty. The man on the left stares happily out at us, the balloon shape stated in his head, his eyebrows, his eyes, and cheeks, even in the sides of his collar. He smiles in a galvanic, hypnotized way. War is exciting, gives you something to read in the papers, something to think about beyond the dull care of life.

His companion, no less mad, is also a balloon man in the inflated sweep of his hair and, again, the round, staring eyes. Together, the two citizens represent the two kinds of madness involved in popular support for war. On the one hand is the all but total idiocy in thinking modern war somehow equivalent to mythical encounters between armored knights on the tournament field, a contest of strength and skill in which "our boys" can show their mettle. On the other is the citizen simply stunned by the prospect of war but unable to recover from the first impact of the new condition of life. In both cases, the citizen is effectively removed from rational thought about the situation of war and worlds away from forming an independent opinion.

"We are mad": the masters have been mastered by their servant.

Face à face . . .

Face to face . . .

The military doctor, inspecting the basic material of war, is also inflated, but not like a balloon, more like some swollen structure of masonry or concrete. He is a blockhouse, as we see in the granular texture of his uniform, related to the granular texture of the wall behind the two. By contrast, the civilian up for examination is made only of weak flesh, flesh made to be prodded and punched, scrutinized not too closely and graded, as in a slaughterhouse, as fit for consumption.

The civilian is neither a robust physical specimen nor a youth in the first flush of patriotism. Thin, even gaunt, the subject of inspection wears the weary look of one who has lived with the war for some time already. This is not the first military call for manpower. The better material has been exhausted.

Ever since the expulsion from Eden, man is humiliated at being naked in the presence of another who is clothed. With this profound and immediate humiliation, military service begins its forced course in reducing the citizen from his native humanity to a more serviceable subrationality. The realization and acceptance of this course is shadowed in the face of the naked man. He stands here humiliated in his frailty before the armored corpulence of the man of death.

But Rouault was not creating an antimilitarist tract. The citizen stands for his examination at the end of a series of events for which he, too, is responsible. He is face to face with the necessities of his own hatred.

Omens . . .

Without at all looking for it, the naked man in the preceding plate unexpectedly stumbled into truth, truth about his situation and his probable future, truth about his own nature, out of which came dismal present and desolate future. Here, in time of war, three gather to seek the truth. The effort is conscious. The desire is to be assured the worst will not befall and that, through whatever difficulties, the seekers will win in the end.

On the right, the lady seer casts her eyes professionally down at the cards she manipulates on the table — or perhaps it is the *planchette* she holds for spirit messages. Overtly, in her downcast eyes and un-enthusiastic face, she makes no great claims for her powers or for the omens her fingers will discern upon the table. She need not. The signs of fortune-telling, like those of the weather, are subject to im-mediate, fulsome, and grateful interpretation by those for whom the signs, the auguries, are invoked.

The young man on the left presents an unmarked face. Experience has written nothing there for him or others to interpret. Nevertheless, head thrown back, hand raised, he dictates to the world of spirits what it is the world of spirits must dictate back to him.

Between these two, between the smooth, modest efficiency of the professional purveyor of the future and the naïve arrogance of the youth ordering tomorrow as he might order a meal, stands the woman who is all of us confronted by war and the future. She is puzzled and she is frightened, both at the vastness of the unknown and at the possibility that it will be known.

PLATE FORTY-TWO: *"Bella matribus detestata."* (Horace, *Odes I, 1, 24–25*)

"War, hated by mothers."

The mother and infant reflect back to the mother and child of Plate Thirteen, "it would be so sweet to love." The two there were close together, almost, as the child's chin fit into the space between the mother's face and her shoulder, the two parts of a complex, interlocking organism. Now space has intervened. Between the two we can see the space of descending night. There is earthly space, marked by the city in the right background. And there is heavenly space, marked by the gentle gradation from the pitch black of the corners to the glowing light that surrounds the pair like a nimbus. Love is the nimbus that surrounds these two. Across the space of war and the thought of war the mother casts the bridge of her protective hand, the child answers with his own hand held up toward the lips of the mother.

Against the background of war on earth — a background provided in the images that have preceded and in those that will follow this peaceful image — the child rears up upon the knees of his mother. His head held high, his back straight, he would be a man. From his own self-sufficiency, the child reaches across space to the mother.

The mother is not such a straight, independent line. The mother is a curve of sheltering love. The curve begins in her pure brow, sweeps back over her head and down her hair, along her arm and hand to hold the child. Behind her smooth brow and betrayed by her reaching hand is her knowledge that to be a man is to go to death.

"Nous devons mourir, nous et tout ce qui est nôtre." (Horace, *Ars Poetica,* 63)

"We must die, we and all that is ours."

The mother holding her child became a single curve of love from her brow to her hand touching the boy. Now, against the murky, stormy background of war, another mother appears, preoccupied with the thought Rouault quotes from Horace: not only must we die ourselves, but all those who are our own must die. Most especially, for this mother, even the child who is not yet born must die. For, as we see in the swell of her body, this solitary woman is curved with life yet to come.

It is a truth of art that there are no straight lines in nature. Straight lines are a convention, invented, like geometry, to impose man's order upon the curving earth and its fullness. A road is straight; a river curves. A building may be made of straight horizontals and verticals; not a hill. Here, in this somber vision of life within life, Rouault reveals curve upon curve. He casts back in his memory to a dress style of his childhood to give this woman the exaggerated shoulders that emphasize the curving nature of her destiny. Her head, too, is covered to make a further, graceful, living curve. Yet, though such head covering and such shoulder ornaments are taken from societies of extreme feminine modesty in dress, Rouault reveals his true intention in the all but total exposure of the life-bearing parts of her body. We are not shocked; we are moved to reverence the swelling hips and belly, the beginning of life. In the swirling murk, lines appear and they, too, curve in echo of life; their velvety black bespeaks the rich and gentle love of motherhood.

But this mother's face recalls the Gospel warning: "Woe to those that are with child in that day."

Mon doux pays, où êtes-vous?

My sweet country, where are you?

We move from the mothers to their sons, slumped here for a moment's rest in the square of a taken town, or a defended town, it hardly matters which. The cry from the heart that is the title of this scene is echoed by every soldier. He is far away from his own sweet country; he is in the strange country of war. The strangeness is but more pronounced if the two happen to be the same, if the country of war has moved into and over the sweet country of a young man's childhood. In either case the friendly and familiar are gone; in their place, even on streets one has walked for years, are the dangerous and the unknown.

How simply and how powerfully Rouault states all this and much more. Six or eight buildings are enough to make the town a reality and they are made with no great eye to detail or variety. On the left, in a row, are houses very much like one another, each with a single door and two windows. On the right and nearer is a taller building. Near the center is a tower. There is, in fact, very little evidence of destruction, yet the whole feeling of place is charged with desolation. There are the two fires, mounting into a sky that continues the effect of the smoke. The sky seems scratched at and raw, in vivid contrast to the velvet background of the pregnant mother. Here darkness is the edge of the earth against the sky and that horizon line is broken by the two pillars of flame.

More tellingly the soldiers are disposed about the public square in positions unthinkable under any circumstances but those of war. The setting is one for peace, for buying and selling the fruits of earth or of skill, for talking with neighbors, for walking to church. Now all action stops. The soldiers wait and, glad to wait, drop where they halt, to rest.

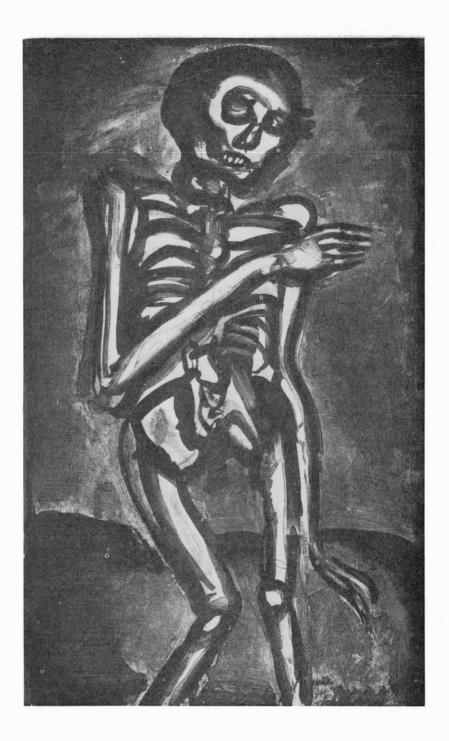

PLATE FORTY-FIVE: *La mort l'a pris comme il sortait du lit d'orties.*

Death took him as he rose from his bed of nettles.

Rouault now begins a suite of deaths, for death is the first thing that happens in war. The figure of death, the skeleton from the ancient European woodcuts, reappears, glistening white against a black sky and a black earth.

The death figure is less jaunty than when he first appeared, in the scene of the soldier telling his sins "for the last time." This is a more sober death image, and he moves across an utterly barren land. Even death, the grinning and jesting death of the late Middle Ages, the death seen in the sweep of the Plague from end to end of Europe, even such a death is surfeited by the slaughter of modern war. The figure moves with a certain reluctance, obedient to its nature but far from the grotesque alacrity of the historical bone man.

This bone man is not only death but also death's victim, rising from his "bed of nettles" to die. There are times when death seems a blessing and is openly spoken of as a blessing. Such a time can come in war and the weary combatant will welcome the bullet or the shell fragment that not only ends his endless calculations as to the day of his death, but ends, too, the daily need to move, to lie down, to get up, to walk, to be weary, to try to kill.

119

PLATE FORTY-SIX: *"Le juste, comme le bois de santal, parfume la hache qui le frappe."*

"The just man, like sandalwood, perfumes the blade that cuts him down."

The mother and child now are reunited to their husband and father — in death. The woman and the boy stand sorrowing at the feet of the just man struck down by the blade of war; at his head and heart an angel attends, who shall speed him to his rest.

The segmented body of the just man, dead, is not unlike the bone composition of the death figure in the preceding plate. Even as the skeleton seems to be pieced together of bones, so this man seems pieced together of individual parts, the limp arms attached to the sections of the torso, these in turn attached to the lifeless legs. Something of this quality of death repeats itself also in the mother and child, perhaps even in the angel. The just man does not die alone. When he dies, those who are with him, physically, or at heart, die also with him.

From the illuminated scene of death, the composition leads our eye, as if up a corridor, toward the doorway; although the interior of the doorway is dark, beyond it light appears. The day may be about to dawn, the end of war, the beginning, once more, of sunlight and growth.

Meanwhile, above the scene, hovers again the true image of Christ on the veil of Veronica. The just man perfumes the human war that kills him and in his death he acquires the mark of Christ, given to one who lays down his life for his friend or for his country.

121

PLATE FORTY-SEVEN:　*"De profundis . . ."* (Ps 129:1)

"Out of the depths . . ."

Through this sequence, as, indeed, through the entire series, the meaning of death emerges from the study of death, the viewing of death in one setting after another. Now the physical scene of the preceding plate is repeated. The angel and the mother and child have gone. The dead or dying soldier, the just man, is alone with death and with the image of Jesus from Veronica's veil, now come forward and shining more brightly. Many of us have seen this moment.

There is still a wall between the dead man and the world. The wall, again, is dark at its edges and around the edge there is light. But now the light is filled with figures. They comprise, perhaps, a parliamentary or diplomatic scene. Far from the field of battle, the diplomats carefully construct an arrangement for ensuring the balance of a peace or a different one for changing the balance of the war; or, the parliamentarians meet to discuss what is to be done, how the war is to be ended or to be pressed on to a victory. In either case the talkers imagine themselves to be in the very thick of the experience of war and are, perhaps, already making notes for their books of memoirs about their war years or their part in the trials of their country.

They are not at the center. The dead man is dead center in the experience of war. Composed in death, he lies calmly beneath the approaching Christ of glory, shining from the veil in answer to man's plea: "Out of the depths I have cried to Thee; Lord, hear my prayer."

PLATE FORTY-EIGHT: *Au pressoir, le raisin fut foulé.*

In the wine-press, the grape was crushed.

Now there is no wall and no world beyond a wall. The world is before us, compressed into shallow space. It is occupied entirely by the "grapes" of suffering humanity, to be pressed, by suffering, into that wine which is the blood of Christ.

The floor of this world is the rigid, horizontal body of the dead in the war that is never ended. Above, there presses down the heavy shadow of night, of death. In the center of the scene, the living oval face stares out in resigned realization of the crushing that takes place in life. To the left, another such oval bows before that fate. But in the face of the man who is both the crushed grape and the floor of the press, there is more than resignation. His face is vertical still, the movement of hope and of life. He waits in calm acceptance for the final pressure which will crush the individual human life into the life-giving stream of wine.

On this comparison between the crushed grape and the man sacrificed, between the wine of life and the blood sanctified, rests the whole structure of the Christian revelation. In Christianity, the cup of wine and the piece of bread of the Sabbath evening have been transformed into a new Sabbath of God Himself as the sacrificial meal.

Through the acceptance of suffering, even the smallest of military factors can become a part of God's sacrifice through the human madness of war.

PLATE FORTY-NINE: *"Plus le coeur est noble, moins le col est roide."*

"The more noble the heart, the less stiff the neck."

Now appear, in series, five faces of war.

The first is the Prussian warlord. He seems a caricature of that East German breed, but in practice the Prussian officer always managed to caricature any caricature of his behavior. Later in the century, the Nazis were to reduce the stiff image to travesty that would have been farce except that so many millions of the innocent went to inhuman death, not even as accidental victims but as victims sought out for slaughter by the stiff-necked and basehearted.

For France in the late nineteenth and early twentieth centuries, the danger of death always loomed in the East, across the Rhine, and this is the form that danger took. Generation after generation of Prussian officers devoted their lives to perfecting plans of destruction to be followed, detail by detail, through Belgium into France, across Poland into Russia, through Bohemia and Austria, down the Balkans to the Black Sea. Any modern — or ancient — powerful state maintains such planning, but in Prussia and in the Germany Prussia dominated, the spirit of such planning shaped the state itself and, through the state, the entire society. This is why, to this day, the Germans are feared and distrusted by their neighbors. Yet today a Germany stripped of its eastern provinces knows a general welfare it never dreamed of as a military power plotting conquest in all directions. How could so much intelligence have been so evilly misdirected so long?

Here we see why. The stiff neck holds the face and the eyes permanently away from human reality, permanently turned to a heaven of one's own choosing.

PLATE FIFTY: *"Des ongles et du bec . . ."* (Guillaume de
Salluste, 1st week, 2nd day)

"With nails and beak . . ."

Here, the second face of war, is the heaven the stiff-necked murderer
turns his eyes toward. Here is the goddess of war, prepared to rend
the enemy with her nails and with her teeth. The goddess proves her
divinity by acting the wild beast.

The Jew's or the Christian's idea of God is often more reflective of
the person holding the idea than it is of independently existing Divinity.
The principle applies with even greater force to gods and goddesses of
pagan pantheons. We recall the goddesses of the ancient Mediterranean,
embodying such things as love of man for woman, the purity of virgin-
ity, the fruitful earth, and wisdom itself. Here is a goddess of the North,
with nails and beak.

The face is cool and dispassionate, utterly without pity. The breasts
have been flattened and hardened; they appear as plates of armor. We
are not surprised that such a goddess should have been created centuries ago by savage tribes roaming the marshes and bogs of Eastern
Europe and nibbling at the edges of the Empire-Civilization of the
South. Nor should it surprise that this chill goddess may still be
worshiped by a humanity still ready to make war.

129

PLATE FIFTY-ONE: *Loin du sourire de Reims.*

Far from the smile of Rheims.

The third face of war is the face of the soldier who must actually do the things that look so ingenious and overpowering on the war maps. Arrows and X's, solid bars and circles must finally be translated out of their aesthetic abstractions and into flesh and blood, a good deal of blood as things have invariably turned out. Here is the flesh.

The recurrent shock in the armistices of man's war with his own kind is the shock of discovery that the enemy — feared, hated, sheltered from, evaded, pursued, battled against — is much the same as oneself. Above all he is the same in his dislike for war. This German soldier wears the same stiff collar as does his master two plates back. But while for the master the collar is a mere adornment of the stiff-necked spirit, for the soldier the collar is a kind of yoke, holding his head high, causing him to suffer, but not finally breaking his painful communion with his fellowman. His decorated helmet sits on his head like an old pot, incongruous, about to fall off, as are his spectacles, reminiscent of the German passion for learning, not at all appropriate to an iron man spreading terror in the world. His eyes, lost without their lenses, and his apple cheeks proclaim his bewilderment at finding himself a scourge and monster.

"The smile of Rheims" is worn by the lovely Gothic angel of the Annunciation on the cathedral there. The cathedral, along with others, was severely damaged by German artillery during World War I.

Rheims is an ancient city and has always attracted barbarian conquerors, beginning with Clovis, who was baptized there. At his throat this soldier wears the cross so many armies use to reward anti-Christian action.

131

Dura lex sed lex.

The law is hard, but it is the law.

Another face of war, and again it is the face of a man who bears the main burden of the battle. In soldier's cap, this soldier of mature years presents his weary, enduring face to the line of pure darkness that advances on the right. But this soldier presents his face not in the blind pride of the German general, not in the trembling bewilderment of the German soldier, but in patient resolution. The law is hard, life is hard, but it can be borne and it must be borne: it is the law.

If it were possible to look at this shape before us and shut out of our minds the fact that this is the shape of a man's face, we would probably take it for a rock. This head is held as a rock of granite is held in earth. From such granite, defensive walls are built to hold back the floods of barbarism. From such granite, also, the men of France of old taught themselves to make cathedrals, like the one at Rheims.

Such elaborate structures, which look like dreams and are made of the heaviest, most solid material, are able to lift themselves above the plains and hills because of the operation of intricate laws, the beautifully named laws of stress and strain. Stresses and strains are evident in this face of war, but because they are subject to the law of man, the man does not crack. Burdened with his personal stress, burdened with the strains of his society, he nevertheless sets his face against invasion from without or from within, and civilization endures because he endures.

Vierge aux sept glaives.

Virgin of the Seven Swords.

The last face of war is the face of the Virgin Mary, protector of France, true Queen, for whom the cathedrals were built.

The seven swords of Mary are, in an ancient devotion, the seven wounds inflicted on her heart during the Passion of her Son. With an instinct too profound for words, the earliest mourners for the grief of the Virgin saw these wounds in a mother's heart as equivalent to wounds made by swords, choosing for their symbol that weapon which, to the pre-Christian states, was noble and which, to the majority of Christian princes, has been no less noble.

As with the soldier in the preceding plate, the face of the Queen of Heaven is turned, unsmiling but not breaking, toward whatever horror may come next.

Mary suffered with the breaking of her Son's Body. But the Body of Christ comprises the whole of the Church, including all those who have been baptized in the spirit through their desire to walk in God's ways. Therefore the thrust of the seven swords and the turning of the blades in the wounds go on throughout human history. As the Passion of Jesus endures through man's inhumanity to man, so does the suffering of Mary, confronted with the endless tearing of the Mystical Body of Christ by its own members.

"Arise, you dead!"

The last movement of the Dance of Death reverses the first. The call of Death is answered by the call of Life. Like Lazarus the dead come forth from their graves. On the black horizon, rows of crosses seem to stir, too, as if animated by the coming dawn after so long, so dark a night.

The three bone men rise from the smothering earth in sequence, as if they are the same man in the process of resurrection from war's death. On the left, the dead man rises from the ground, skull lifted up curiously, bone fingers raised tentatively toward air and life. The second man steps awkwardly up and out upon the surface of the earth, so long and so heavily pressed down upon him. At the same time, he sways backward, hand pressed to mouth in awe, unbelieving, even unwilling to believe the long night of death is over. The third man, wearing the soldier's cap in which he died, returns to life with confidence fully restored. He accepts the new life and moves forward to its challenge. He raises his arm in a gesture of leadership. Although he has himself responded to the cry, he also seems to have given it: "Arise, you dead!"

Resurrection from death takes place at the end of time. It takes place also on the occasion of the individual's death, when he confronts his own soul in judgment. In the crucible of war, resurrection may take place from the death of insensitivity, the death of cruelty, the death of normal, human egotism. All suffering presents the opportunity for such a resurrection. In the suffering of war the dead may rise in the individual's final determination to offer his own life for something outside himself.

137

PLATE FIFTY-FIVE: *L'aveugle parfois a consolé le voyant.*

Sometimes a blind man has consoled the seeing.

In contrast to the bone men, these two survivors of war are fleshed out and move through the dawn-lighted land as toward their home in their own country.

One head is up, the other down. We have seen this combination before, on city streets, the blind man led by his friend who can see. Now the parts of the combination are reversed. The blind man, his eyes mere black patches turned to heaven, steps forward humbly but confidently in the belief that his foot will fall upon the right path and stumble no more. His sighted companion, eyes cast still upon the earth, holds his arm, content to be led, grateful to be led in the new country of resurrection from man's wars and deaths, a country so new that even vision from the old world is useless here.

The blind man, having lost that old vision, walks in the new country like a native.

PLATE FIFTY-SIX: *En ces temps noirs de jactance et d'incroyance, Notre-Dame de la Fin des Terres vigilante.*

In these dark times of vanity and unbelief, Our Lady of Land's End keeps watch.

Almost every sea-bordered country has a coast, a cape, a promontory which those who live there call "Land's End." In France such a place is Brittany, jutting into the cold Atlantic. Rouault's father came from Brittany and that ancestral connection is here remembered and made into a symbol of the human situation. Whatever our country, however far we live from the coast and the crash of waves, we live at Land's End, *La Fin des Terres*.

On the right, the silhouette of the land declines sharply to where it would end and meet the sea. On the left, more gradually, the land does the same thing. But out of the meeting of these two declining headlands, where shadow would meet shadow and sink into the sea, just there the Virgin Mother, Our Lady of Land's End, rises like the crudely carved image of humble piety. From that end of earth, she rises like a flower, washed by the sea, nourished by the land, and radiating her own pure light. In the gloom of "these dark times," Our Lady and her Son send forth their rays to hold, for us, the night at bay.

Upon the firmly rooted body of the Virgin rests the eternal circle of Mother and Child. The movement begins in her head covering and in her eyes downcast in love; proceeds through her shoulder, her arm and hand, where it is taken up by the body of the Child. It sweeps up again as His head bends toward hers, but the circle is closed in His hands holding our world held out to her.

141

PLATE FIFTY-SEVEN: *"Obéissant jusqu'à la mort et à la mort de la croix."* (Phil 2:8)

"Obedient unto death and to death on the cross."

Yet, though He holds the world in His hand, He enters the world, suffers the world, and dies in the world, for the world. This theme returns constantly throughout the *Miserere,* as it does throughout the history of Christianity, and as it does throughout the life of Christ.

The one thing Rouault says over and over and never tires of repeating is this: Christ did not die once and rise to glory in a strange land long ago. He dies and dies and dies every day in every land in the presence of every soul that ever lived. In that Death is our salvation. In the acceptance of our own daily deaths, we join Christ on the cross. Being human, we are born to suffer whether we will or not. Through Christ's example, we can suffer in Him and in His Spirit, accepting what we cannot change and helping others where it becomes possible.

This image of the Crucified stretches the arms and the torso as on a rack of torture, inclines the head as in increasing pain. Yet the face is calm in the radiating light of total love.

143

"C'est par ses meurtrissures que nous sommes guéris." (Is 53:5)

"It is by his wounds that we are healed."

And at the end, once more the "true image" of Veronica's veil, the image drawn by an act of love in the midst of an act of death.

The cloth itself is present in the oblong outline; yet the cloth fades as we confront that image. Here is the face of Christ beaten and bruised, nailed to a cross and lanced, taken down dead and buried, risen in three days and gone before us into glory. We see a hint of the Beatific Vision, of Jesus in eternity, having lost none of the marks of agony, yet changing them all into a richness and beauty that survives all worlds.

At the end of his own long struggle to imagine, to create, and to bring to the light of day this tremendous Christian testament of faith, Georges Rouault addressed a preface to his work, completed at last, and concluded:

"Jesus on the Cross will tell you better than I."

SUGGESTED BOOKS

Georges Rouault MISERERE, with a preface by the artist and an introduction by Monroe Wheeler (New York: The Museum of Modern Art, 1952).

Art and Scholasticism, with other essays, Jacques Maritain, translated from French by J. F. Scanlan (New York: Charles Scribner's Sons, 1946).

The Woman Who Was Poor, Léon Bloy, translated from French by I. J. Collins (New York: Sheed and Ward, 1947 [original, 1897]).

We Have Been Friends Together, Raissa Maritain, translated from French by Julie Kernan (New York: Longmans, Green and Co., 1942).

Georges Rouault, James Thrall Soby (New York: The Museum of Modern Art, 1947).

Rouault, Lionello Venturi, translated from Italian by James Emmons (Paris: Skira, 1959).

Georges Rouault, Pierre Courthion (New York: Harry N. Abrams, Inc., 1962).

Georges Rouault MISERERE, with a preface by the artist and introduction by Anthony Blunt and a foreword by Isabelle Rouault (Boston: Boston Book & Art Shop with the Trianon Press, 1963).

NOTE

Original prints from the MISERERE can be seen in many museums and galleries. In addition, they may be seen in the following schools, to which Leonard Scheller, a Milwaukee newspaperman, has given individual prints and groups of prints:

St. Louis, Missouri
1–58, St. Louis University

Milwaukee, Wisconsin
3, 36, 42, 52, Marquette University
3, 7, Cardinal Stritch College
21, 55, Alverno College
3, 55, Mount Mary College
47, Pius XI High School

Omaha, Nebraska
3, 36, 55, Creighton University

New Orleans, Louisiana
32, 55, Loyola University

Mobile, Alabama
32, Spring Hill College

Denver, Colorado
55, Regis College

Notre Dame, Indiana
36, St. Mary's College

Chicago, Illinois
3, 55, Loyola University

West De Pere, Wisconsin
22, St. Norbert College

Chestnut Hill, Massachusetts
55, 58, Boston College

Syracuse, New York
3, Le Moyne College

New Haven, Connecticut
13, Albertus Magnus College

Webster Grove, Missouri
3, Webster College

Washington, D. C.
20, 36, Georgetown University
22, Dunbarton College

Canton, Ohio
36, Walsh College

Fond du Lac, Wisconsin
30, Marian College

Mequon, Wisconsin
47, Notre Dame of the Lake
Motherhouse

Cedar Rapids, Iowa
6, Mount Mercy College

St. Paul, Minnesota
47, Nazareth Hall
Preparatory Seminary

Woodstock, Maryland
30, Woodstock College

149